THE DEBACLE OF ECONOMIC STABILIZATION POLICIES

How Central Bankers and the Government Wreck the Economy

Antony P. Mueller

Copyright © 2018 by Antony P. Mueller. All Rights Reserved.
Paperback edition ISBN: 9781731202208
All rights reserved. No part of this book may be reproduced in any form or by any electronic or mechanical means including information storage and retrieval systems, without permission in writing from the author. The only exception is by a reviewer and by academics, who may quote short excerpts in a review.
Printed in the United States of America

based on "Beyond the State and Politics. Capitalism for the New Millennium"
First Printing: April 2018
Amazon KDP
New edition July 2018
ISBN-9781980571445
also available as e-book

THE DEBACLE OF ECONOMIC STABILIZATION POLICIES

CONTENTS

- Introduction
- The myth of crisis capitalism –
- Stagflation -
- Say's Law -
- Monetary policy -
- How small crises become big crises –
- A menu of models –
- Survey of business cycle models –
- No crisis without a boom -
- What happened in the Great Depression? -
- Lessons yet to learn -
- Misery Index -
- The economics of inflation and deflation –
- The sorrows of central banking –
- Inflation-targeting –
- Bailouts and stimuli –
- The pitfalls of policy-making -
- The value of money -
- End the Fed –
- The crisis of 2008 -
- Summary

List of Figures and Tables
Bibliographical references

Antony P. Mueller

"ALL THAT A GOOD GOVERNMENT CAN DO TO IMPROVE THE WELL-BEING OF THE MASSES IS THE ESTABLISHMENT AND PRESERVATION OF THE INSTITUTIONAL FRAMEWORKS THAT DO NOT HINDER THE ACCUMULATING OF NEW CAPITAL AND ITS USE TO IMPROVE THE TECHNICAL PRODUCTION METHODS."
LUDWIG VON MISES: 'PLANNING FOR FREEDOM' (1952)

THE DEBACLE OF ECONOMIC STABILIZATION POLICIES

The declared goal of macroeconomic policy is to stabilize the economy. This claim implies the assumption that the market economy is inherently unstable. Yet what if it is not the market economy but politics which produces instability? What if when the policy managers fabricate the opposite of their claim? What if when they do not flatten the business cycle but make it more extreme? What if when monetary policy does not cure inflation but instigates the erosionof the purchasing power of money?

The great economic eruptions happen when the government and the central bank do not allow the small economic fluctuations to play out. The authorities hinder the return to a balance when false incentives and distorted market signals persist. When capital becomes scarcer, the interest rate should rise to signal this change. If, however, the central bank attempts to pump more money into the systems and to lower the interest rate, this policy will cover up the capital shortage. Cheap credit insinuates a profusion of funds that do not exist.

Economic policy claims to stabilize the economy and keep it on its growth path. For that purpose, economic policy is said to fight inflation and deflation, to prevent recessions and depressions and to promote economic growth. Yet, often, these policies themselves produce the disasters that the policymakers claim to prevent and to cure.

Antony P. Mueller

THE MYTH OF CRISIS CAPITALISM

The business cycle comprises the ups and downs of economic activity. One must distinguish between fluctuations - the slight oscillations of the economic process - and the strong waves of the boom and the bust. The term 'cycle' - if it should evoke the image that the economy swings regularly between expansion and recession - is inappropriate because there are no regularities in the movements of economic activity. Each stage, be it recession, stagnation, or depression, can last for a long time. There are countries that do not escape their economic standstill, and there are those economies, which enjoy a good economic performance for decades, and experience only brief and slight dips or no recession at all for a long time.

The Marxists put the myth into the world that extreme crises were inherent to the market economy when in fact, the strong economic fluctuations have come from war and political unrest, or by natural events and acts of God, and are not due to the inner workings of capitalism. War, revolution, civil war, ethnic, and religious conflicts have been the main causes of economic collapse, long-lasting stagnation, and failed recoveries. Throughout history, it has been politics that has ruined the economic well-being of the people.

For the 20th century, one can say, all the evils of that century followed from the basic error of expecting to improve the human condition through politics. If we want to avoid similar catastrophes in the 21st century, we must stop politics and dismantle the state.

The Great Depression, which dates from 1929 to 1939 for the United States, but that began in Great Britain already in the early 1920s, was the consequence of the First World War and the world-political conflicts after the duplicitous Treaty of Versailles. It took until after the end of the Second World War until the Western nations could find their way back to cooperation again.

THE DEBACLE OF ECONOMIC STABILIZATION POLICIES

In Eastern Europe, the stagnation continued after the end of World War II because the Soviet Union imposed its socialist system on the countries that the Soviet leader Stalin gained with the consent of the British Prime Minister Churchill and the US-American President Roosevelt at the Yalta Conference in February 1945.

Western Europe received the American Marshall Plan from 1948 until 1952 and helped to launch the European recovery. The 'economic miracle' of the recovery of the Federal Republic of Germany in the post-war period is only partly the result of the Marshall Plan. Just as important was the program of economic liberalization that Ludwig Erhard (1897-1977) started with his monetary reform in June 1948. Yet towards the end of the 1960s, Germany, too, resorted to an activist economic policy.

Nowadays, there is little tolerance to the natural fluctuations in the economic process. Even the natural swings of the economic activity lead to exaggerated reactions of economic policy. The fear is that even a small increase in unemployment would cost the government its reelection. Yet by not allowing the natural fluctuations, economic policy earns the big fallout.

This way, the economic stimulus measures of the 1960s laid the foundation for the inflation in the 1970s and the excessive reaction to the stock market decline at the start of the new millennium led to the crisis of 2008.

In Japan, the central bank stimulated the excessive boom of the 1980s. When the crisis came 1990, neither expansive fiscal nor monetary policy helped to get the Japanese economy out of its slump - despite the size and duration of the measures. The massive fiscal and monetary stimuli to fight the downturn of 2008 has not produced a swift recovery but laid the groundwork for an even worse crisis.

The graph shows the long-term trend in the US economy of an increase in per capita income of 1.87% per year since 1789 and the projection from 2013 to 2088 of a growth rate of 1.6% per year. The major economic fluctuations in the 18th and 19th centuries resulted from war and domestic conflicts such as the Napoleonic Wars, the American civil war, and the wars of independence.

The 'Great Depression' is the most pronounced deviation from the trend. The crisis was longer and deeper because of the false monetary policy of the Federal Reserve System and the many economic policy errors of Franklin Delano Roosevelt (President of the USA from March 4, 1933, to his death on April 12, 1945).

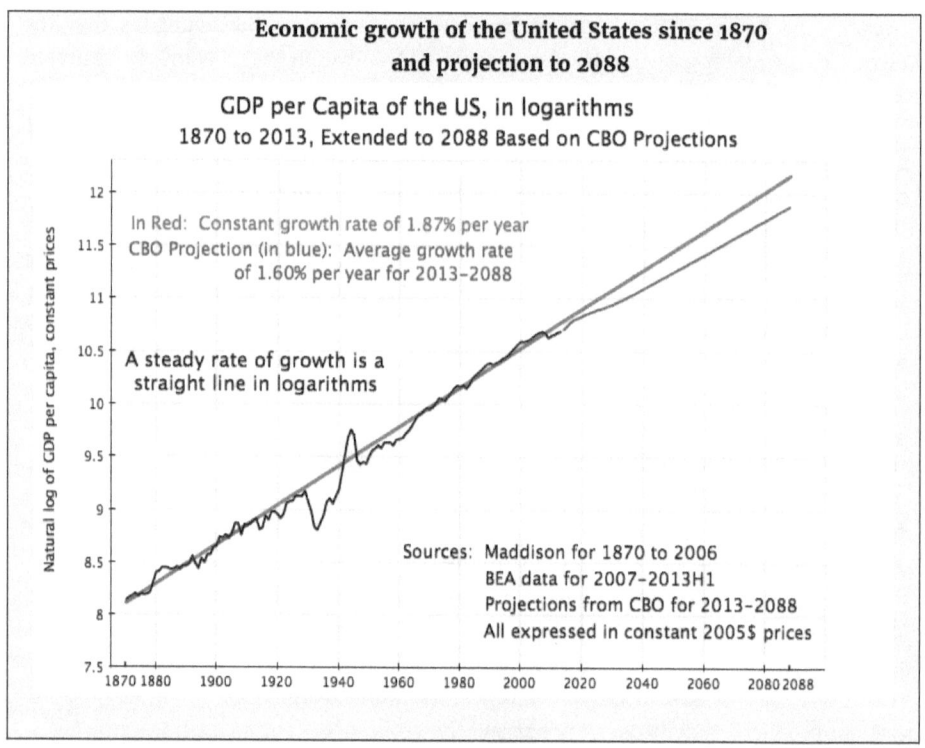

The boom of the post-war period came after Roosevelt's demise when a pro-market orientation of the American economic policy took hold. Yet things changed later again towards interventionism in the 1960s and in the 1970s. The 1980s and the 1990s saw respite, but since the start of the new millennium, monetary policy has become expansionist without being able to stimulate economic growth. Debt accumulation and interventionism demand their toll and have pushed the U.S. economy from the 'Great Moderation' into the 'Great Recession' that has become the 'Long Stagnation'.

***

In the United States, the welfare state, whose foundations came into existence during Roosevelt's New Deal of the 1930s, experienced a revival in the 1960s and continues its expansion since then. After the 1962 Cuban crisis and the assassination President John F. Kennedy in 1963, the hot phase of the Vietnam War began under the presidency of Lyndon B. Johnson (U.S. President from 1963 to 1969). With the Vietnam war, the welfare state grew at high rates in this period.

The American central bank, together with the other major central banks, helped to support this expansion of government expenditure with a loose monetary policy under the spell of the cheap money cult. When, during the war in the Middle East in October 1973 (the 'Yom-Kippur War' - from 6 to 25 of October 1973), the group of oil exporting countries (OPEC) launched a boycott of the supply of crude oil, the simultaneous occurrence of recession and inflation brought about the stagflation of the 1970s. Attempts to stimulate the economy through public expenditure programs combined with easy money failed. The economies did not recover despite massive government spending combined with strong monetary stimuli. What increased, was unemployment, the inflation rate, and government debt. The economic policy followed a Keynesian orientation. This economic doctrine, laid down by the English economist John Maynard Keynes (1883-1946), states that one must overcome an economic crisis by more government spending and more easy money.

STAGFLATION

The term 'stagflation' signifies the combined appearance of stagnation and inflation. In the 1970s, all major industrialized countries suffered from low growth, high rates of price inflation, persistent underemployment, and widening budget deficits. In the United States, both, the price inflation rate and the unemployment rate, reached double digits in the 1970s and early 1980s.

Source: http://multiplier-effect.org/a-cautionary-note-about-stagflation-in-the-1970s/

The dominant macroeconomic policy theory in the mid-1960s until the end of the 1970s was 'Keynesianism', according to which an economy is in the state of a 'deflationary' or an 'inflationary' gap.

Keynesian diagnostics and its economic policy toolkit

A deflationary gap comes along with a falling price level and rising unemployment. As the Keynesian theory diagnoses these phenomena as the result of a lack of demand, the government must apply expansive monetary and fiscal policies. In contrast, thus says the Keynesian doctrine, an inflationary gap results from an excess of demand which leads to inflation and over-employment. Here, the right policy is a fiscal and monetary contraction.

Confronted with stagflation, the Keynesian policy knew no answer. While doing away with unemployment would require expansive policies, fighting inflation would need contracting measures. Additionally, the Keynesian policy paralyzed in the face of stagflation because high unemployment and stagnant growth meant widening budget deficits and a mounting public debt.

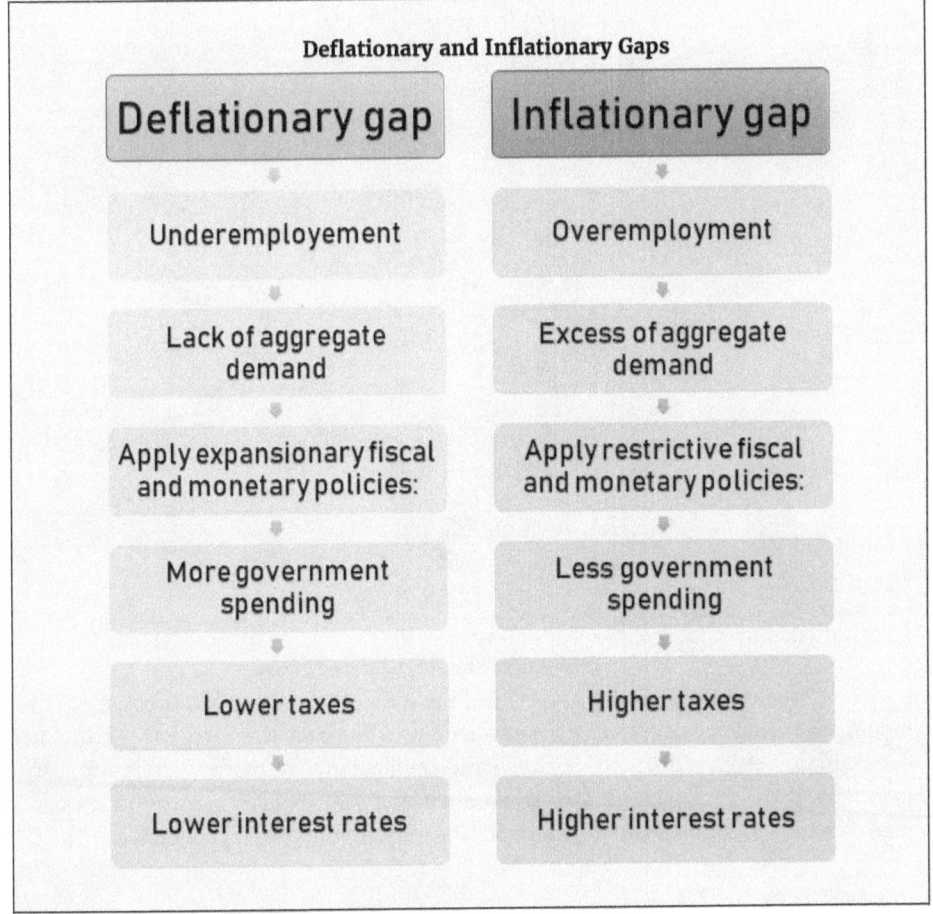

The principle of Keynesianism states that the government expenditures should not come with a balanced government budget, but that the extra spending should happen through borrowing. With the credit-financed expenses, the state assumes budget deficits. The doctrine says the government should spend in place of the consumers and of the companies to overcome the investment weakness and the consumer restraint in the private sector. The problem with this theory is that it cannot explain why, after all, there was a falloff in investment activity in the first place.

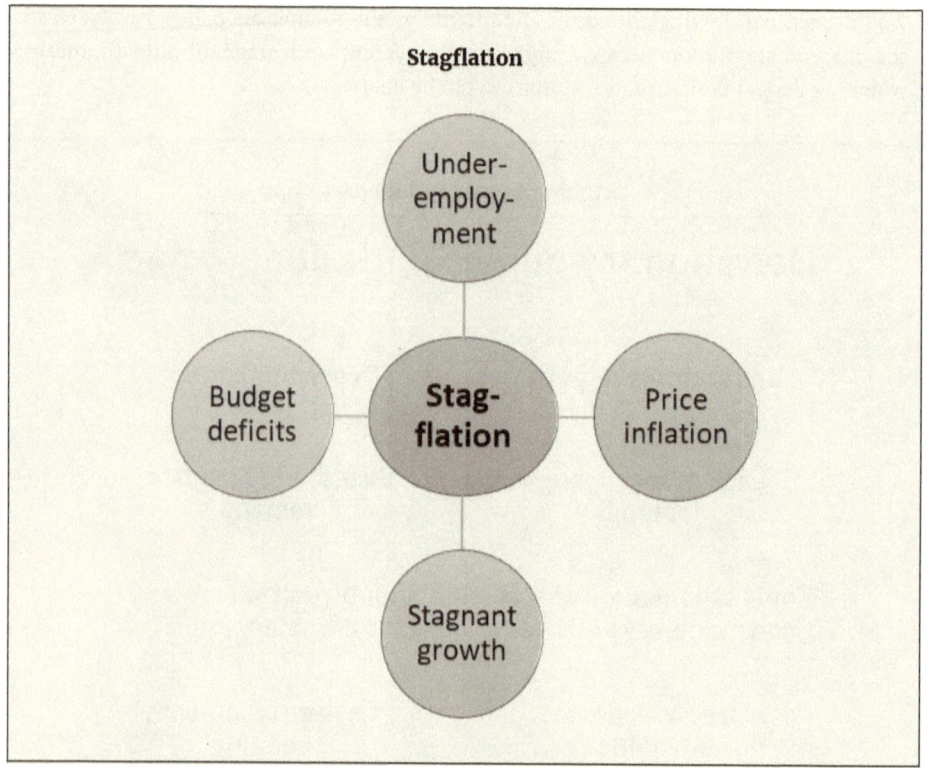

Defects of the Keynesian Theory

The Keynesian theory suffers from a series of fundamental problems. The model makes no clear distinction between the short and the long run as to the determinants of investments (long run) and the demand for money (short run). An insufficient distinction refers also to nominal and real variables. If the Keynesian model wants to explain unemployment, the model requires real variables. Then, however, additional government spending cannot expand the economy at will. More spending is not equal to real economic growth.

The Keynesian model cannot explain the breakdown of 'animal spirits' as the cause of the fall of investment and as the trigger to the business cycle. Extreme levels of aggregation conceal more than they reveal and a mechanistic interpretation of cause and effect between the variables makes the Keynesian model unrealistic.

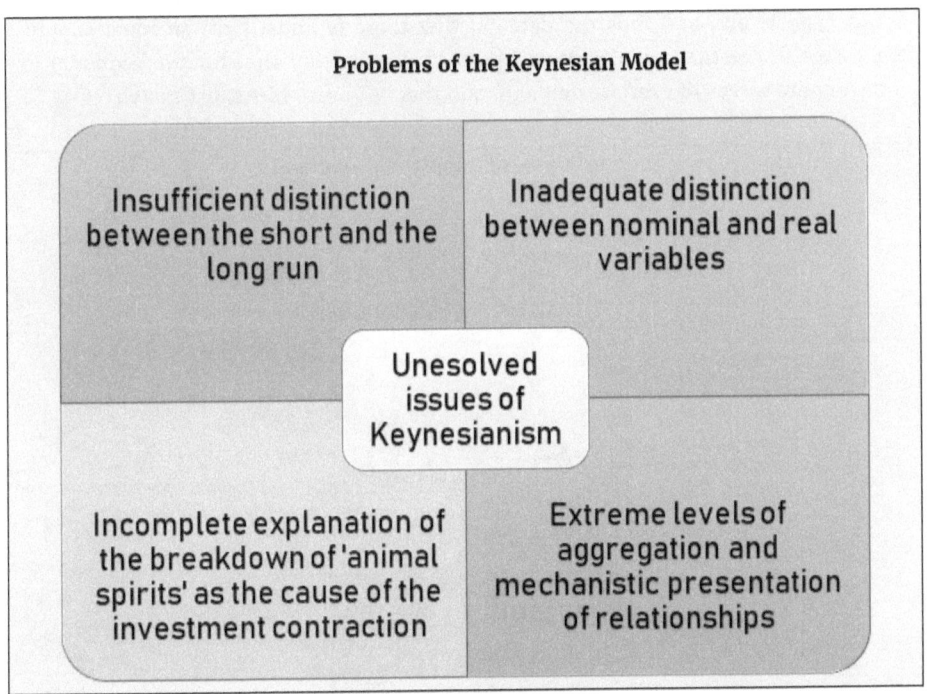

***

The economic model of the Keynesians postulates that aggregate demand determines economic activity. Therefore, the policy recommendation says that if there is insufficient private demand, the public sector must jump in. With this theory, Keynesianism stands in contrast to classical economic theory according to which the growth of an economy depends on the production. For the classical economists, production generates the means demand goods, as stated by 'Say's law'. According to the classical theory, economic crises show that technical innovations or changes in consumer preferences or the political and social environment require restructuring the economy's supply side.

Say's Law

Keynes and his followers distort 'Say's Law'. They claim it says 'supply creates its own demand' when in fact the theorem denotes the law of the market, which contends that supply equals demand and that to exercise demand one must have something to offer. Because for the economy a whole, credit and financial assets cancels out, and thus the demand that there is, must have an equal supply. Say's Law is not that supply creates its own demand but that for the economy in total, supply serves to exercise demand, and that both variables must match.

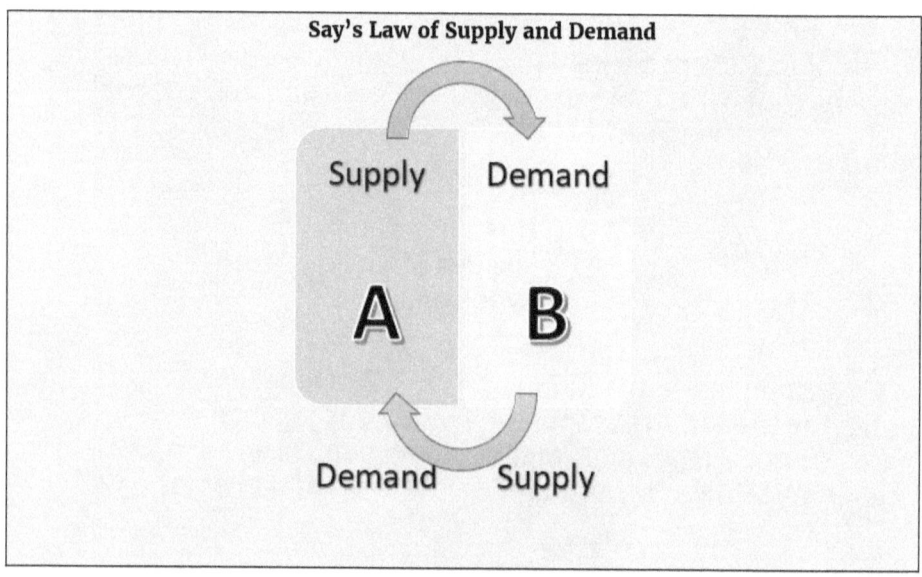

In a market economy, there cannot be an 'over-production' and an 'under-consumption' as the Marxists and their Keynesian followers claim. If a company produces an item that it cannot sell at the expected price, it must lower the price. When the price falls below the marginal cost of production, the company suffers losses and consequently must abandon producing this good. This happens all the time with individual companies and specific goods. If it were not so, business would be an easy game.

The Marxist term of 'under-consumption' signifies that workers would produce more than they earn. Yet this claim does not hold for a competitive market economy. As long as the remuneration of a worker is below its marginal revenue product, a company will increase its overall profits by hiring more workers. A firm will stop using more workers at the point where the marginal revenue product of labor equals the wage rate.

As long as the wage rate is below of what labor contributes to the sales revenue of the product, a company will hire additional workers and stop when the two rates are equal. When the wage rate exceeds the revenue product of the workers, the firm must lay-off labor until the two rates will be equal again.

Determinants of Employment

Wage rate below marginal revenue product of labor

- → **Hire workers**

Wage rate is above marginal revenue product of labor

- → **Fire workers**

Equilibrium condition:
Wage rate = marginal revenue product of labor

A frequently used argument says that when companies dismiss workers, the overall volume of demand will shrink and thus the slump will deepen. The answer to this claim is that if wage rates do not fall to the level of productivity, business would make losses and inhibit capital accumulation. Yet capital accumulation along with technological progress must take place to lift productivity up to the wage level and to do away with unemployment. There is no other way but dismissal when the wage rate is too high because if the workers stayed in their jobs, they would provoke losses and thus inhibit the capital accumulation. Profits are a necessary condition of capital accumulation and a wage rate in tune with labor productivity is a necessary condition to make profits. Capital accumulation raises productivity and thereby more labor will be employed, and then the wage rate can rise.

***

In the perspective of classical economics, it is not the task of the state but that of the entrepreneurs to redirect the production structure and to adapt the production process to the altered conditions. According to the Keynesian doctrine, in contrast, the economy recovers due to government spending, which stimulates the economic actors to ask for more goods and services. When this happens, so the Keynesian theory says, the economic engine will start again, and the cart moves out of the ditch. One must 'crank up' the economic motor. In order to stimulate the economy, the government must apply 'pump priming'.

At the heart of the Keynesian message lies the psychological thesis that in a crisis the entrepreneurs and the consumers fear spending their money. To compensate for this, the state would have to overcome this paralysis by credit-financed extra expenditures. As demand increases, economic activity would revive because entrepreneurs and consumers would regain confidence and spend more money again.

Three years before Keynes' monograph appeared, Germany's Nationalist Socialist government started a policy of government deficit spending in early 1933. This experiment influenced Keynes' thinking as it proves the English economist's preface to the German edition of his "General Theory of Employment, of Interest, and Money". The General Theory appeared in the English original in 1936 and received a German translation in the same year. In his preface to the German edition, Keynes elaborates that his theory would work better under an authoritarian regime than in a free democracy and that the Nazi economic policy was the first test case for his 'new economics'.

The Keynesian economic model works better under the conditions of a dictatorship than in a democracy because a state-sponsored demand policy requires additional compulsory measures to prevent that the money creation that comes with the government's spending policy would cause the price-wage spiral. The reason the Nazi variant of Keynesianism worked and because the mass unemployment in Germany disappeared without inflation in a few years was that this policy combined strict price and wage controls. After the fire of the Reichstag building on the night of February 27, 1933, the new government put the union leaders, together with leading Social Democrats and Communists, into 'protective custody'. The entrepreneurs, as far as they were loyal to the new regime, became operations managers and had to obey the government directives although private property in its formal legal sense remained intact.

The Third Reich completed the system of state capitalism, which had come into being during World War I and had continued in the 1920s. More radical than the Italian fascism, Nazism subjected the economy and society to totalitarianism. In contrast to the Soviet Socialism, National Socialism was a socialism that maintained private property in its positivist legal sense. Yet National Socialism put the economy also under a plan whose main aim was the military armament. Not only in this respect are National Socialist (NAZI) Germany and the Union of the Socialist Soviet Republics (USSR) twins. Both systems were socialist not only by name.

The circumstances are very different if one wants to practice demand policy under the conditions of a liberal democracy. If government finances its expenditures through deficits, the amount of money that circulates in the economy will increase. If the stock of money in circulation grows faster than production, prices will rise. Higher prices call for higher wage demands by the workers and their representatives. A price-wage spiral emerges. The irritations, which emanate from inflation, along with the ensuing labor struggles about wages and strikes, brings about the opposite of the desired economic recovery. Instead of an economic rebound, recession looms. As the money supply expands in line with the size of deficit spending, the simultaneous occurrence of economic stagnation and price inflation sets into motion.

Price-wage-price-spiral (PWP-Spiral)

An increase in government spending brings with it a monetary expansion, which leads to a higher price level. Price inflation will lead to demands for higher wages, which put further pressure on rising prices. Such a process can go on as long as the central bank aliments the process with monetary expansion. The longer the inflationary expansion last, the harsher will be the effects of the contraction.

The cleavage between deficit spending, price inflation and stagnation became a major topic in the 1970s. The 'stagflation' brought monetarism as an alternative policy concept to the forefront. In the late 1970s and the early 1980s, the industrialized countries tried to put an end to Keynesian policies and replace it with the monetarist 'counter-revolution'. The teachings of the monetarists say the economic cycle depends on the variations of the amount of money that circulates in the economy, and that the best way of practicing economic policy is keeping the money supply steady by having money grow at a pre-fixed annual rate.

The main representative of monetarism, Milton Friedman (1912-2006), showed that the US-American central bank prolonged and deepened the economic crisis of the Great Depression of the 1930s. According to his analysis, the US central bank allowed the money supply to shrink and thus price deflation to happen. As a result, real interest rates rose and there was a fall in consumption and investment.

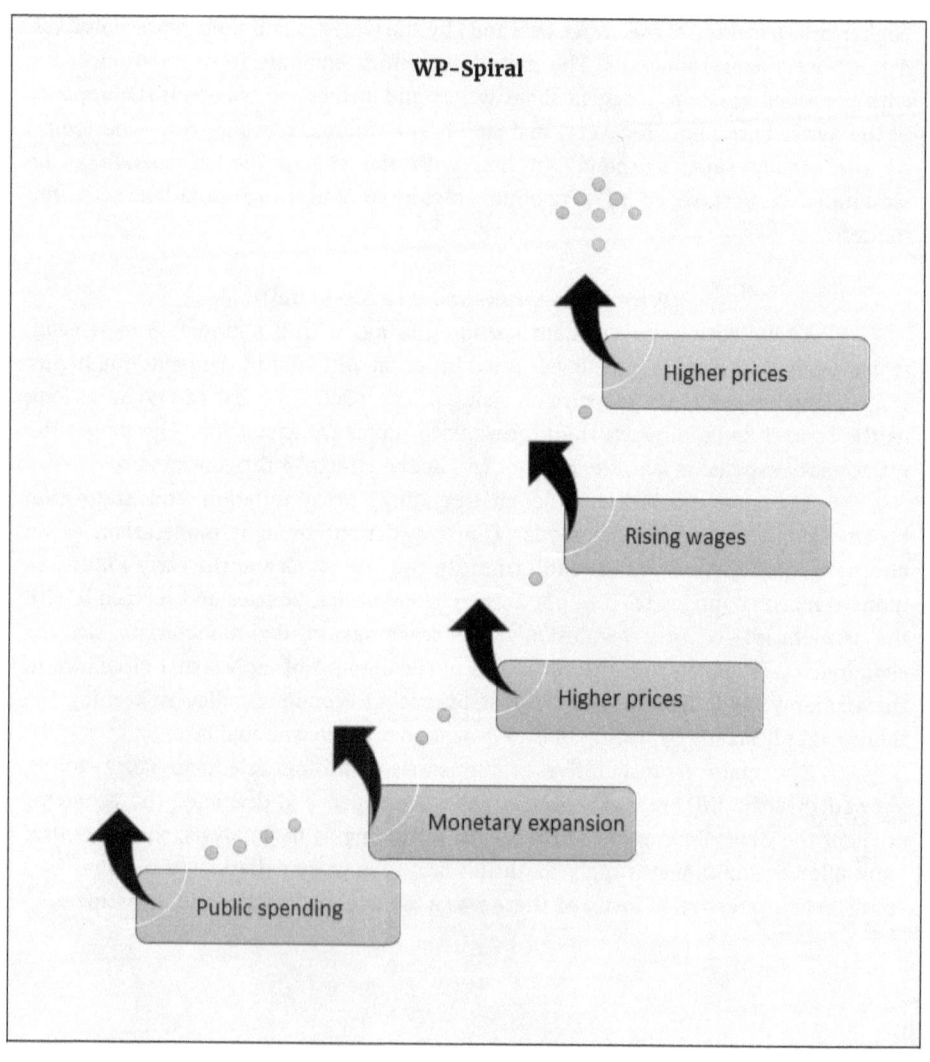

KEYNESIAN, MONETARIST, AND NEO-CLASSICAL MODELS OF ECONOMIC CONTRACTIONS

For the Keynesians, the starting point of an economic crisis, which manifests itself in less production, is a fall in overall demand and the cure exists in stimulating aggregate demand. The policy recipe of the Keynesians is anticyclical government spending.

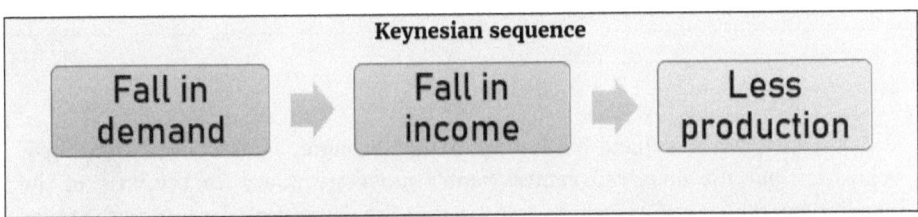

For the monetarists, the starting point of an economic downturn is a monetary contraction, which leads to less spending and to a fall of economic activity. In order to prevent less production, the monetary authorities should take care that the money supply does not contract. The policy recommendation of the monetarists is a stable growth rate of the monetary supply.

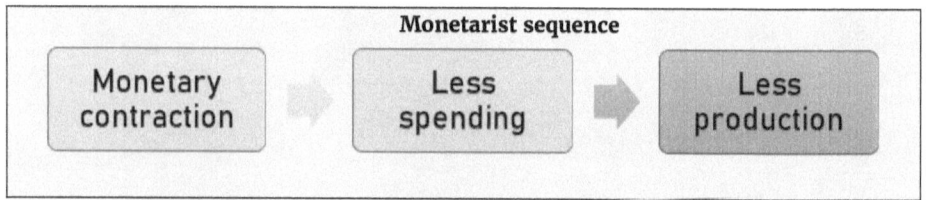

Classical economics explains a downturn as the result when the wages rates exceed the marginal productivity of labor. To forestall losses, companies must dismiss labor, and the economy enters a temporary contraction. After the wage rates have adapted to the marginal productivity of labor, new hiring sets in and the economy moves out of the dint.

The neo-classical sequence precedes both the Keynesian and the monetarist sequence. What these two opposing views take as the cause - the fall of aggregate demand and the monetary contraction - is, in fact, the outcome of a wage mismatch brought about by the trade unions that cooperate with the government.

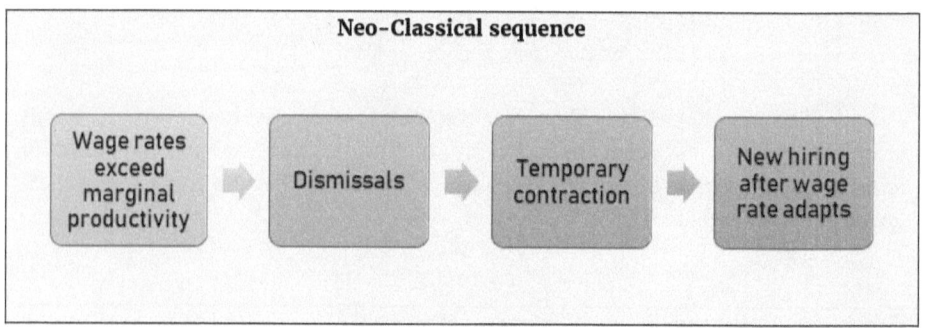

***

Friedman explained that not the market economy is to blame for the Great Depression but the American central bank's monetary policy. In the view of the monetarists, the lack of aggregate demand that the Keynesians deplore as the cause of the Great Depression was the fault of the monetary policy of the American Federal Reserve System (FED) and not a failure of the market economy. What the Keynesian diagnose as insufficient aggregate demand was a monetary contraction.

Yet Friedman ignored in his analysis that the Federal Reserve had committed two errors. It pursued a false policy not only because it was too restrictive in the crisis, but also because it was too expansive in the 1920s. By heating the boom in the decade preceding the Great Depression with low-interest rates, the FED prepared the path to the crash. American monetary policy instigated both: the boom and the subsequent bust.

From the 1960s onwards, monetarism gained influence in academia and replaced the Keynesian explanation of the crisis. The stagflation of the seventies gave Keynesianism its deathblow because their macroeconomic demand model was incapable of explaining how recession and inflation could occur at the same time. By the late 1970s, monetarism became a mainstay of monetary policy.

When the US inflation approached the fifteen percent mark towards the end of the 1970s, the time had come for a monetary policy turnaround. The President of the United States, Jimmy Carter (President from 1977 to 1981), appointed Paul Volcker as the chairman of the American central bank. Volcker took office in August 1979 and implemented a monetarist policy. During 1980, the US central bank, under the new directorship, conceived the monetarist experiment, which comprised shifting from the focus on the interest rate to the control of the money supply.

Defects of monetarism

The monetarist model establishes a relation between the money supply and the price level. According to the monetarist doctrine, rising prices come about when the money supply expands too much.

To reduce the rate of inflation, the rate of the increase of the amount of money in the economy must diminish. As a practical policy model, four questions arise:

First, which criteria fit the definition of the money supply to calibrate the monetary policy's interim policy aim? Second, which is the relation of the monetary aggregates (M0, M1, M2, M3, etc.) to the monetary base? Third, which is the appropriate monetary aggregate that the central bank can control? Is the management of the monetary base sufficient to control the other monetary aggregates? Fourth, how works the transmission mechanism in detail? What are the links from the money supply to the national income and to the price level? How does the monetary aggregate, which serves as the central bank's steering tool, affect the other monetary aggregates, the interest rate, investment, and consumption? Finally, how does money and the price level impact on the real gross domestic product and on employment?

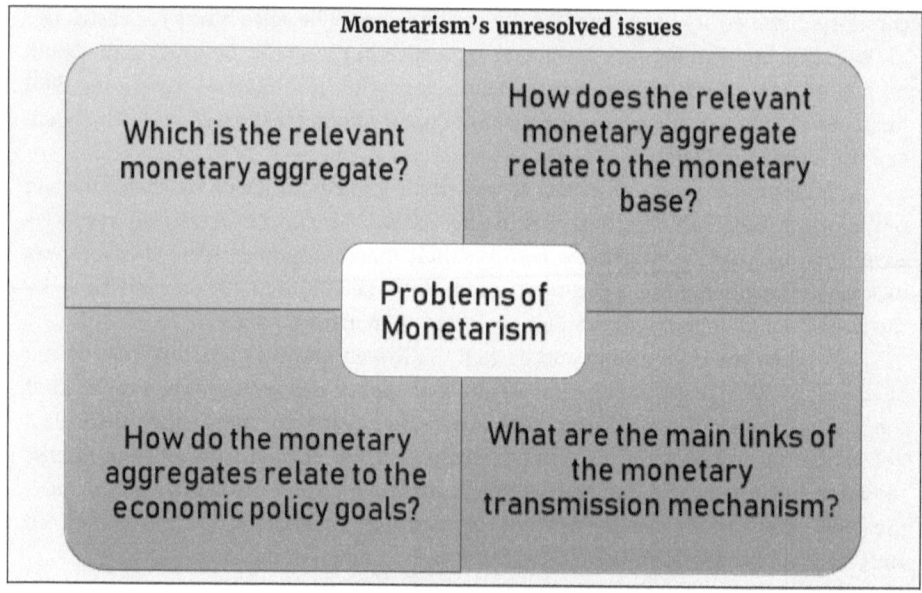

***

When the American central bank under Paul Volcker's chairmanship designed the new monetary policy, the experts knew of the causes of the Great Depression as due to monetary contraction. The policymakers at the FED knew of the risk of pushing the economy into a depression if the money supply should shrink too much. Therefore, the monetary policy aim was to avoid an abrupt contraction and not to provoke a recession or a new depression.

To plan a monetarist policy operation and to determine the monetary target, the monetarist policy projection must include the expected velocity of circulation in its calibration. As of 1980, the statistical data showed a continuous increase in velocity. For the several decades before 1980, econometric analyses established an almost perfect trajectory of the velocity of money. This way, so it seemed, the future rate of the velocity of transactions was to project with high confidence and one could put the number into the equation to expand the money supply. On these considerations, the US central bank decided upon a monetary target which corrected the rise of the money supply by the expected increase in circulation. Because the rate of velocity was rising, the amount of reducing the quantity of money had to fall more than otherwise to compensate for the increase in velocity. It came as a big surprise when the statisticians of the US central banks discovered after some time that as soon as the new monetary policy began, an abrupt change of the trend of the velocity of circulation had occurred. Instead of continuing to rise, the velocity of money had fallen. The planned moderately restrictive monetary policy turned into a strong contracting policy.

As a further irony of the story where one more error offsets another error, came into play that Ronald Reagan (President from 1981 to 1989), as the newly elected president, wanted to augment the defense budget. As the increase in spending requires to calculate in real terms, the estimated inflation rate played an important role to determine the size of nominal budget increases. In 1981, when preparing the first Reagan budget, none of the budget experts assumed a rapid decline of price inflation., which was around ten percent. Together with the other budget items, the projected defense spending rose by the desired real increment plus the compensation for the expected inflation rate. Public expenditure in real terms rose much stronger than intended when the rate of inflation fell more than expected. The following recession was deep but short. As a legacy remains the inception of a new cycle of higher national debt together with the myth that celebrates Paul Volcker as the daring inflation fighter. Inflationary expectations vanished from the system without a long-lasting recession not because of a superior policy design but by accident. The good performance of the U.S. economy in the years to come came as the result of the double error of a fiscal policy that was too expansive and a monetary policy that was too restrictive.

MONETARY POLICY

The 'Monetary History of the United States, 1867-1960', written by Milton Friedman with Anna Schwartz and published in 1963, identifies the monetary contraction as the cause of the Great Depression. The depression was deep and long because the US central bank did not counter the squeeze of liquidity with an appropriate increase in the money supply thereafter.

Friedman developed the concept of a quantitatively oriented monetary policy. According to this concept, monetary policy must not focus on the interest rate, but on the money supply. According to the monetarist doctrine, an increase in the price level, i.e. price inflation, results from expanding the money supply that exceeds the real growth of the economy. Therefore, a policy of combating inflation requires diminishing the rate of expansion of the money supply and in the more severe cases of inflation to reduce the absolute amount of money that circulates in the economy.

An indispensable premise for the practice of monetarist policy requires that the velocity of money would be constant or trend stable or that one could preview the price increases by some other prognostic technique. Yet if the velocity of money changes its course over time, these changes are not foreseeable, and the monetarist monetary policy will fail.

Velocity of circulation

The velocity of money refers to the frequency of transactions in an economy. One unit of money can serve for several transactions. The velocity of money can thus strengthen the effect of a change of the amount of money either to an expansion or to a contraction. Inflationary expectations lead to a rise in the velocity of money while deflationary and dis-inflationary expectations lead to lower velocity of transactions.

A monetarist monetary policy must fail if the velocity of the circulation of money is not stable. The effects of the variations in the money supply are unpredictable because one cannot foresee how the velocity of money changes. The trends often last a long time and then change abruptly. A reliable calculation of the future trend is not possible even if for the past many data points are available which seem to suggest a stable trend.

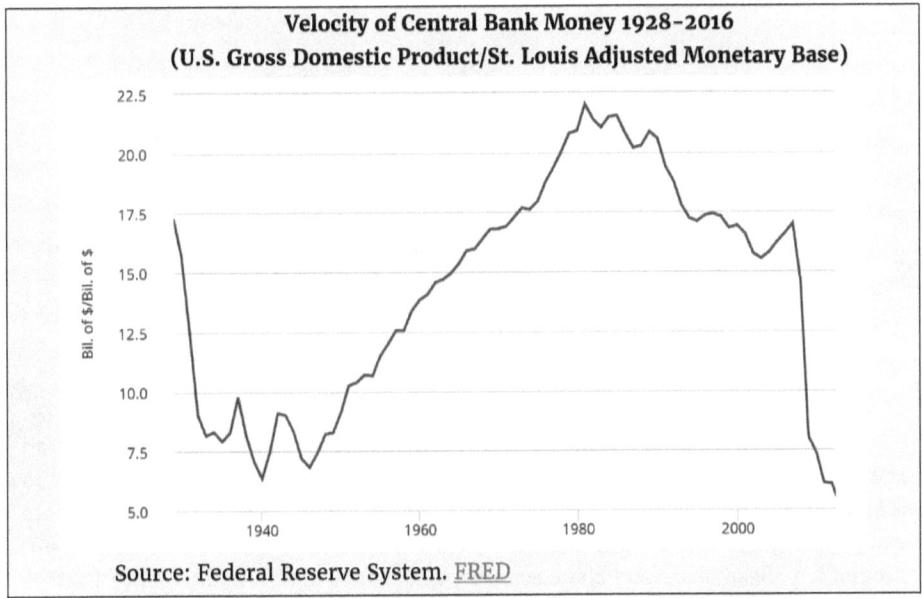

Source: Federal Reserve System. FRED

The graph shows the velocity of money (Nominal national income divided by the monetary base) from 1928 to 2016.

One can see the collapse of the velocity of money during the Great Depression and the long period of the increase of the velocity from the 1950s until 1980 before the trend turned and the further decline of the rate of velocity that happened since the outbreak of the international financial crisis in 2007. The contraction of the velocity of circulation of money explains why the massive increase of the monetary base by the American central bank as a response to the financial crises has not increased the price inflation.

The downturn in the 1980s occurred after the American central bank had introduced its new monetary policy. It turned out that the measures taken were far more restrictive than intended. The U.S. interest rate rose, and the American economy plunged into a recession that dragged many of the indebted developing countries into insolvency. The deceptive relationship between the money supply and nominal gross domestic product before 1981 induced the American central bank to launch a much more restrictive monetary policy than it had planned.

Antony P. Mueller

HOW SMALL CRISES BECOME BIG CRISES

Many people still hang on to the naïve belief that the economy needs an active policy to function, and that monetary and fiscal stimuli are necessary to achieve economic growth, 'full employment' and a 'stable' price level. Governments and central banks still stick to the concept of macroeconomic demand management. Economic policymakers and the electorate ignore that the economic policy itself is often the reason for economic weakness and unemployment and that monetary policy itself is the main cause of price inflation. Under the conditions of the current system of governance with its party democracy, those politicians gain most support who preach activism and promise to realize the impossible.

Although the macroeconomic demand theory is dead, it continues to live on as vulgar Keynesianism at the policy level. Since the economic downturn in the early 1990s, Japan has been trying to resolve its economic crisis with the quackery of a policy aimed at stimulating aggregate demand. Right from the start of the recession, the Japanese government began with a series of expenditure programs to boost the economy. The Japanese central bank has pushed interest rates into negative territory, but the economy has not much recovered. In the meantime, the Japanese government debt has grown in dimensions that otherwise only occur in times of war. This policy has been a gigantic waste.

The immense sums that the government spent over the past quarter of a century did not help to lift the Japanese economy out from its stagnation. What remains of this policy is a vast debt overhang, which has paralyzed private economic activity. Savings are in decline, fears of coming tax increases are on the rise and the innovative zest has faltered. Among the top industrialized countries, Japan has become the country whose economy has experienced the sharpest decline in productivity increases since the 1990s.

Stagnation has become a permanent feature of the Japanese economy. Instead of fostering a swift recovery, the Japanese economic policy has made the structural distortions of the economy more rigid. Macroeconomic policy since the 1990s has wasted much of the wealth that Japan had accumulated in the decades after World War II.

The Case of Japan

The graph below shows the policy interest rate of the Japanese central bank (solid line with the figures on the left scale) compared to the Japanese debt ratio (dotted line with the figures on the right scale).

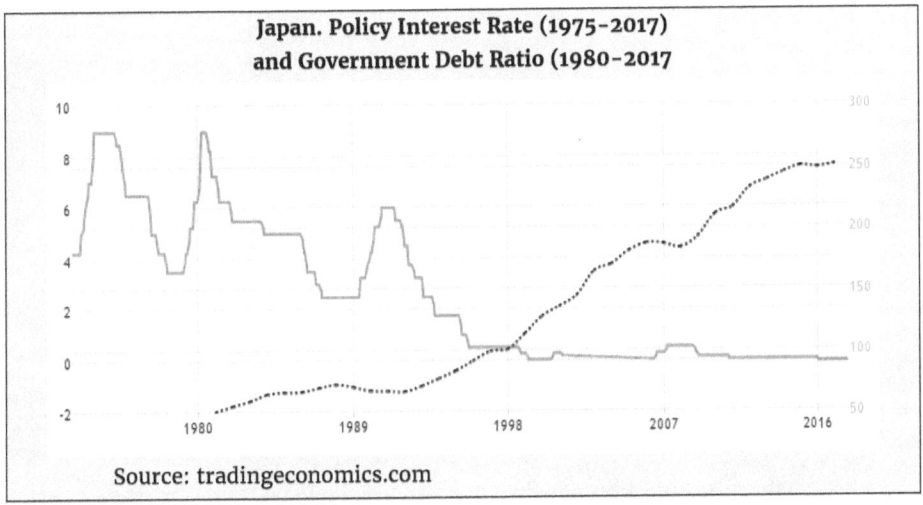

By the end of 2016, Japanese government debt had reached 250% of the gross domestic product. Since the mid-1990s, the debt ratio has risen by 150 percentage points since the start of the low-interest rate policy of the Japanese central bank - which put its key rate close to zero and, in some periods, even into the minus territory.

The result of these massive stimulus packages that led to quasi-zero interest rates and a debt ratio of 250 percent was not only that Japan did not get out of the slump but also that its productivity rate, which had been in line with the other important industrialized countries until the 1990s, began to slump as well.

The data show that Japan has been falling behind since the middle of the 1990s and enjoys less productivity per working hour than Italy and the United

Kingdom and that Japan suffers from a big productivity gap with the United States, France, and Germany.

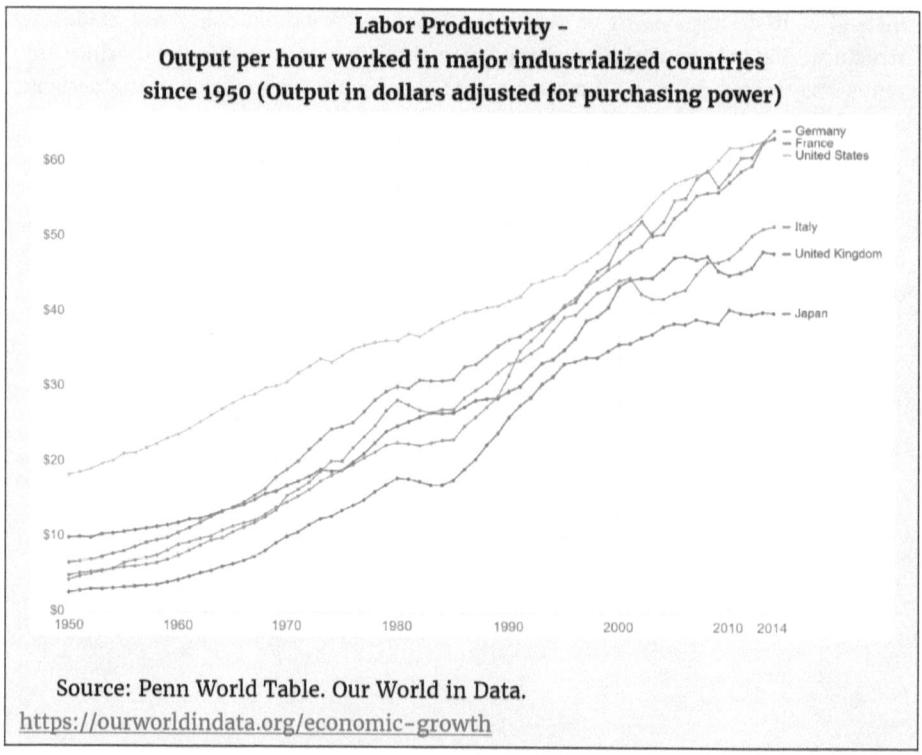

Source: Penn World Table. Our World in Data.
https://ourworldindata.org/economic-growth

Neither the American nor the European economic policymakers have drawn the right lessons from the Japanese disaster as the reaction to the 2008 crisis documents. In the USA and Europe, central banks have cut interest rates and governments have expanded government spending. Yet these measures have not led to a solid economic upturn.

Although Keynesianism is no longer a leading paradigm in academic economics, governments continue to follow its recipes with blind enthusiasm. Politicians favor Keynes' economic policy concept because it suits them well to justify spending and thus any sign of a recession legitimizes higher government debt. Yet while governments are exploiting economic downturns to increase government spending, they have a hard time to tackle the nation's debt burden. No government wants to ruin its chances for re-election because of an increase of the interest rate, higher tax rates, and cuts in government spending, in particular for 'social' purposes. Governments follow the rule that the pain should come later while the pleasure is for now.

While the original theory of government deficit spending would call for anticyclical fiscal policy, budgetary policies follow an opportunistic line. The original theory of Keynes calls for a debt reduction when the economy is doing well. Yet for governments, Keynes has become an alibi which serves to justify extending the state's activities and to accumulate more debt in good and in bad times. Different from what Keynes envisioned, the national debt rises during a recession but does not fall when the economy is expanding.

Public debt cycle

Keynes' trust in the rationality of the state was so deep that he believed governments, which would boost public debt as deficit spending in the bust, would reduce the debt level in times of the boom. This way, John Maynard Keynes presumed the long-term debt level would remain constant.

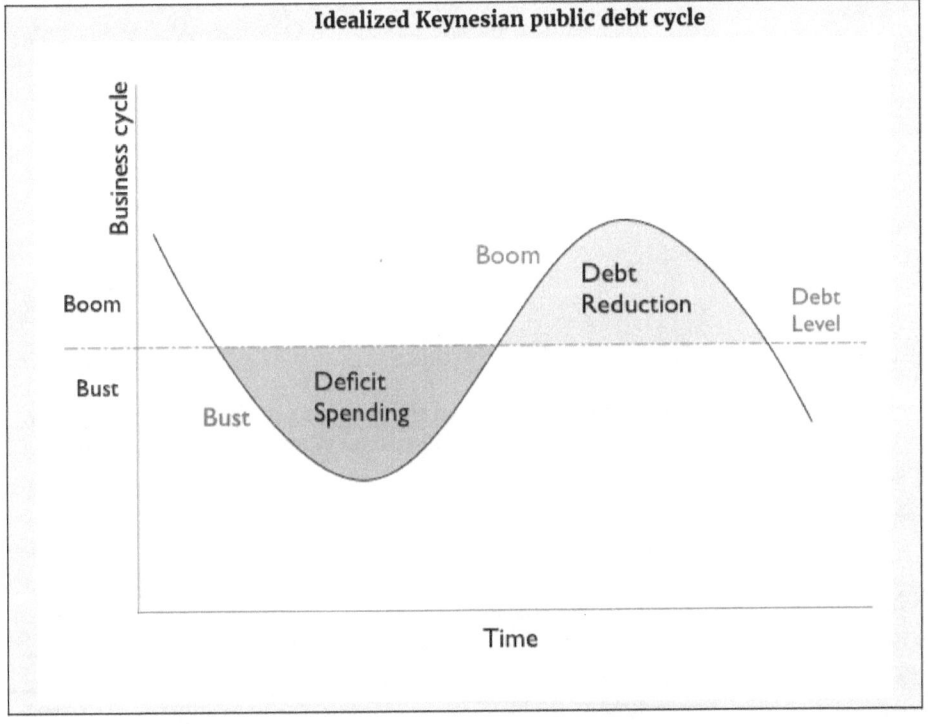

Things worked out differently. While governments took the Keynesian rationale to boost government spending in periods of the bust, they did not reduce public debt when the economy was doing well. This way, there has been a steady rise in public debt. Along with the demands as they come from healthcare and old age in particular - there is the ratchet effect of rising public debt that comes from boosting government spending in an economic crisis while not reducing debt when the economy booms.

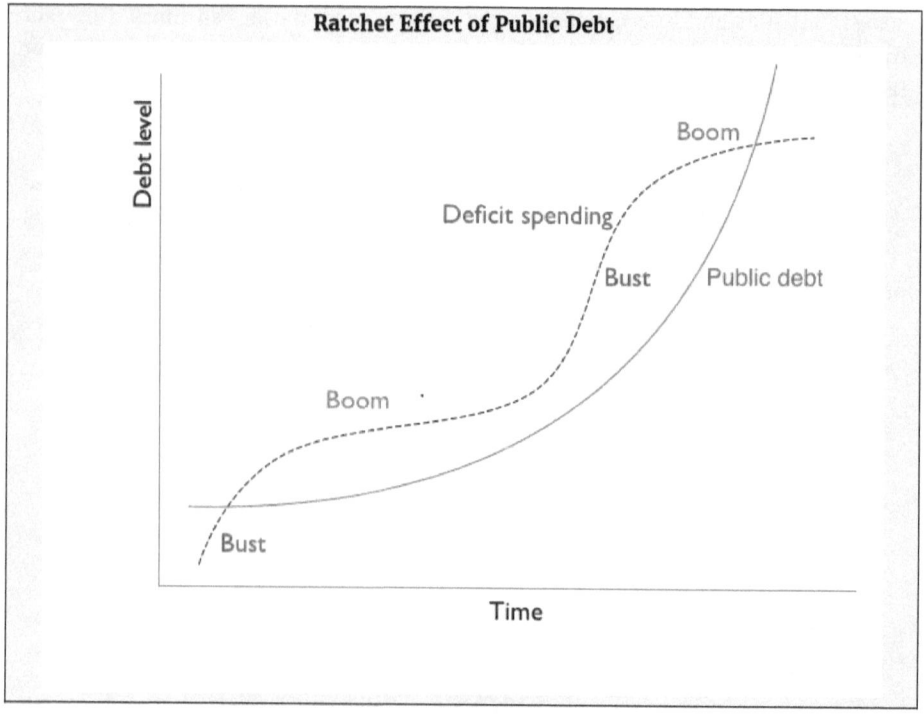

The leading industrialized countries are practicing a failed economic policy. As a result, the economies experience slow growth, and the productivity and the wage rates have stagnated, while public debt is on the rise. Almost all the economic progress that has occurred over the past decades was the result not of these countries' own economic policy but came from the economic liberation in Eastern Europe and Asia. The economic reforms toward a market economy of many countries that had adopted socialist regimes have led to creating many large new trade areas. One of the big beneficiaries of this development was Germany whose economic performance improved as the country developed close trade relations with the countries of Eastern Europe and Asia where reforms in favor of capitalism had taken place.

A MENU OF MODELS

Other than as a crude psychology, the doctrine of Keynes cannot explain why the entrepreneurs should collectively cut down investment and cause a recession. Why should businessmen suddenly lose their 'animal spirits'? While it happens frequently that individually the leadership of a company will misjudge the future needs, the thesis that suddenly most members of the business community should lose their drive has no foundation. The crucial point left out by Keynes is to investigate the specific economic reasons investments drop. Instead of postulating obscure psychology, economics must investigate the difference between the fall of investment expenditure because of a shrinking demand when specific goods or certain product lines become obsolete on the one hand and the contraction as a macroeconomic phenomenon on the other hand. In a microeconomic perspective, a good that is no longer in demand on the market makes way for the demand for another commodity as its substitute. There is no fall in aggregate demand. What does the Keynesian theory mean when it postulates the fall of aggregate demand not as a consequence but as a cause for the economic downturn?

For the classical economics, a contraction of demand for the economy in the aggregate is not possible. This 'law of the markets', which goes back to Jean-Baptiste Say (1767-1832), pronounces that producing the goods is the basis for the demand of goods in the exchange process. Total supply must equal total demand. The price mechanism corrects discrepancies in individual markets. The demand theorists, in contrast, use psychology to explain the business cycle. According to the Keynesian view, the moods of businesspersons fluctuate like that of maniacs between anxiety and euphoria. Such a thesis implies that economic actors are not only fools but also lunatics that suffer from chronic manic-depressive afflictions. This comes in handy for Keynes' solution, which is to take economic decisions, particularly those on investment, out of the hands of the private sector and turn the decision-making over to the government.

Keynes regards the state as an asylum of reason, in contrast to the irrational investors who act driven by fear and greed, and the consumers who spend according to what they get. To this day, this message from Lord Keynes delights all believers in the state as a supreme entity beyond the world of the mortals. Brought to its core, the Keynesian psychology postulates that businessmen are psychotic, consumers act like robots, and only government officials act wise, rational, and with foresight. Yet what appears as irrational to the Keynesians is, in fact, a rational reaction to the follies of the government.

Rising government spending and a higher public debt reduce investor confidence and increase uncertainty. The decisions in the private sector may seem irrational yet it is the capricious unpredictability of government decisions that drive the economic decision-makers nuts. Economic policies are a major source of uncertainty as they produce inflation, recessions, and depressions, and most of all, represent a constant source of uncertainty. If entrepreneurs observe that the government and the central bank will apply expansionary demand policy when signs of an economic downturn appear, business will postpone new investments because they can expect lower interest rates, new subsidies, and new tax reductions. To prevent a recession, economic policymakers turn slight economic downturns into deep recessions.

Producing the crisis that government said to cure happened also with the Great Depression. This tragedy was not due to a failure of the free market economy but of government. The Great Depression came about because World War I had wrecked the liberal monetary system of the gold standard and disrupted the system of an unregulated free world trade system. What came out of World War I (1914-1918) was interventionism, protectionism, communism, and Nazism. Toward the end of this bloody conflict, the international Communist movement had found a national power base with the Russian Revolution (1917) and in the Soviet Union (officially founded in 1922), which thereafter threatened the world for the next 70 years.

The First World War has brought with it not only material costs but also a moral and ideological destitution because of a profound spiritual crisis. In the war and afterward, a generation grew up, which had lost their religious faith together with the confidence in the value of individual freedom and the advantages of the market economy. Fascism and National Socialism along with world Communism and protectionism are all children of the same parent, namely World War I. What unites these various ideologies is their anti-capitalism. Theories of classical liberalism with individual freedom and private initiative at its base had to make room for collectivism and state interventionism. No wonder that 'animal spirits' faded in the face of the follies of politics, state, and governments.

Anti-capitalism

While Soviet Communism took a clear anti-capitalist stance, National Socialism was likewise anti-capitalist albeit in a more disguised form. The difference between Soviet Communism and National Socialism is that the Soviet version had international aspirations and wanted to implant a world communism, National Socialism represents the national version of socialism.

Permanent foes of capitalism are protectionism and interventionism. Interventionism justifies its activity as a way to improve capitalism while protectionism claims to protect the citizens against foreign competition. All four anti-capitalist forces are children of World War I.

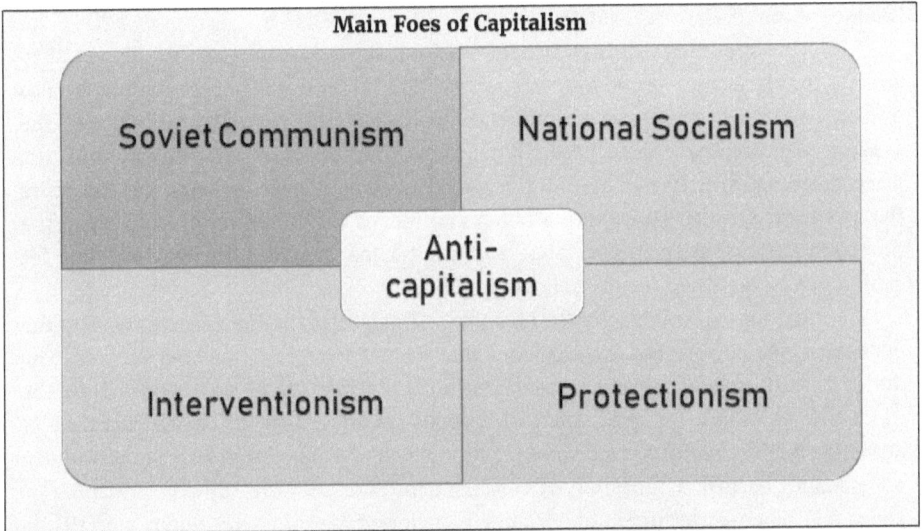

After the neoclassical economic theory had amended the errors of classical economics in the 1870s, especially in value theory, a modern economic theory had emerged at the turn of the century. This new monetary theory identified the banking system as the origin of economic fluctuations. If there is an oversupply of money that pushes the monetary interest rate below its natural level, the economy experiences an artificial boom that will end in a bust.

The natural interest rate reflects the time preference in society, which determines savings and investment. Saving means to forego current consumption to get a higher level of consumption in the future. For the economy to grow, savings must become investment and turn into capital. If, however, the central bank, together with the commercial banks under its authority, expand the money supply and lowers the monetary interest rate, the economic agents take the increased money supply for actual savings when in fact the original time preference has not changed or has even deteriorated.

For the individual company, it looks as if there were more savings available than there are. A low-interest rate deceives about the state of scarcity in the economy and insinuates that it would be possible to realize longer-term and more costly investment projects. Yet when authentic savings have remained at the same level as before, the new projects, which the cheap money had induced, confront a lack of available resources and must be abandoned even before they get completed. The demand of the consumers remains at the former level and may speed up with the pace of the fall of the interest rate. Consequently, demand for investment is rising in tandem with the demand for consumer goods, while both demands clash in the face of insufficient real funds.

The spending for investment and consumption are in conflict as they wrestle for the scarce production resources. The increase in money combined with low-interest rates pushes economic activity beyond the normal utilization of the capacity and creates a false boom. At the onset, prices may not yet rise, and the price-wage spiral may not yet have begun if the wage-level persists. Yet the more the economic activity grows into a boom and moves to the limits of production, the more bottlenecks arise in the labor and capital markets and prices rise, first for capital goods, and then for the consumer goods.

The crisis, which follows the boom, reveals that the investments during the expansion phase were bad investments that do not yield the expected returns. The outlook for their profitability came from the erroneous calculation, which took the monetary variables for real and confounded more money with an increase of authentic savings. A correction requires liquidating the failed projects and the return to normalcy as fast as possible. If this happens, the crisis is solvable and may be short. Yet when government intervenes in favor of 'keeping the boom going', the adaptation does not take place. Failing to cure the wrong investment now lead to even more malinvestments and the costs will be higher when the next crisis comes.

During the process of abandoning the bad investment projects, unemployment rises, demand falls and liquidity contracts. Business must struggle with overcapacities. The profit outlook deteriorates, and some companies must go bankrupt. Financial problems emerge, and creditors lose their assets. Consequently, the offer of credit shrinks. The expansion becomes a contraction and price inflation turns into deflation. It seems as if there were a 'lack of aggregate demand' when in fact correcting the wrong investment projects takes place. While Keynes interpreted the fall of the propensity to invest and to consume as a psychological deficiency, this condition, in fact, is the rational consequence of the economic situation that came because of the policies of the government and the central bank.

In the perspective of the Austrian theory of the business cycle of the neoclassical economic theory, not the recession needs correction, but the recession corrects the false boom. The problem is not the recession, which is the healing process; the problem is the wrong boom because of the expansive monetary and fiscal policies, which the nation's central bank and the government have fabricated.

Antony P. Mueller

SURVEY OF BUSINESS CYCLE MODELS

Business cycle models fall into three categories: models, which see the cycle inherent to a capitalist economy, models, which claim external factors cause the business cycle, and those models, which say government policies are the main cause of the business cycle.

The Marxist, Keynesian and Post-Keynesian theories fall into the categories of endogenous models, while for the New Keynesians, for Schumpeter, and for the Real Business Cycle models, the causes for the business cycle lie outside of the market economy and affect the economy in the form of external shocks.

The third group of policy-induced models blames economic policy as the cause of economic crises. Into this group fall the monetarist, the neoclassical, and the Austrian models of the business cycle.

Typology of Business Cycle Models

Endogenous	Exogoneous	Policy-induced
Marxist	New Keynesian	Neo-classical
Keynesian	Schumpeterian	Monetarist
Post-Keynesian	Real Business Cycle	Austrian

A. Endogenous Models

The Marxist, Keynesian, and Post-Keynesian models postulate that the causes for the business cycle are inherent to the capitalist economy. Consequently, the remedy must be the abolishment of the capitalist system (Marxian theory) or the management of capitalism through macroeconomic policies (Keynesian theory) or by comprehensive regulation (Post-Keynesian theory).

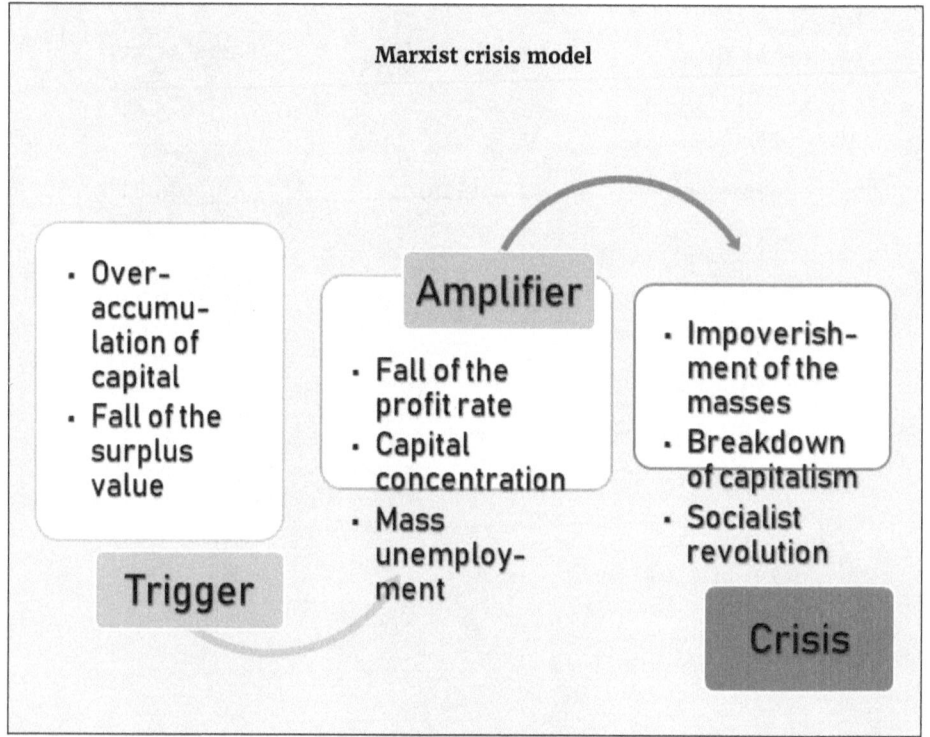

The Marxist theory of economic crises holds that capitalism brings about its own downfall because capitalist competition leads to the over-accumulation of capital and thus to the fall of the relative share of labor. According to the theory of Marx, the so-called 'exploitation rate' is equal to extracting 'surplus value' from the labor force. The profit rate shrinks with the relative share of labor in the production process.

According to the Marxian model, the decline of the surplus value leads to a fall in the profit rate. The concentration of capital increases and mass unemployment follows. Mass impoverishment prepares the collapse of capitalism. The socialist revolution puts an end to capitalism.

Contrary to the Marxian prognosis neither mass impoverishment nor the breakdown of capitalism have occurred. On the contrary. The freer the capitalism, the more technical progress has happened, and productivity increases. With higher labor productivity came rising income. The greatest beneficiaries of capitalism have been the members of the so-called working class, and they know it – different from their self-proclaimed leaders who either by intentions or intellectual deficiency propagate impoverishment and alienation to preach their gospel of revolution.

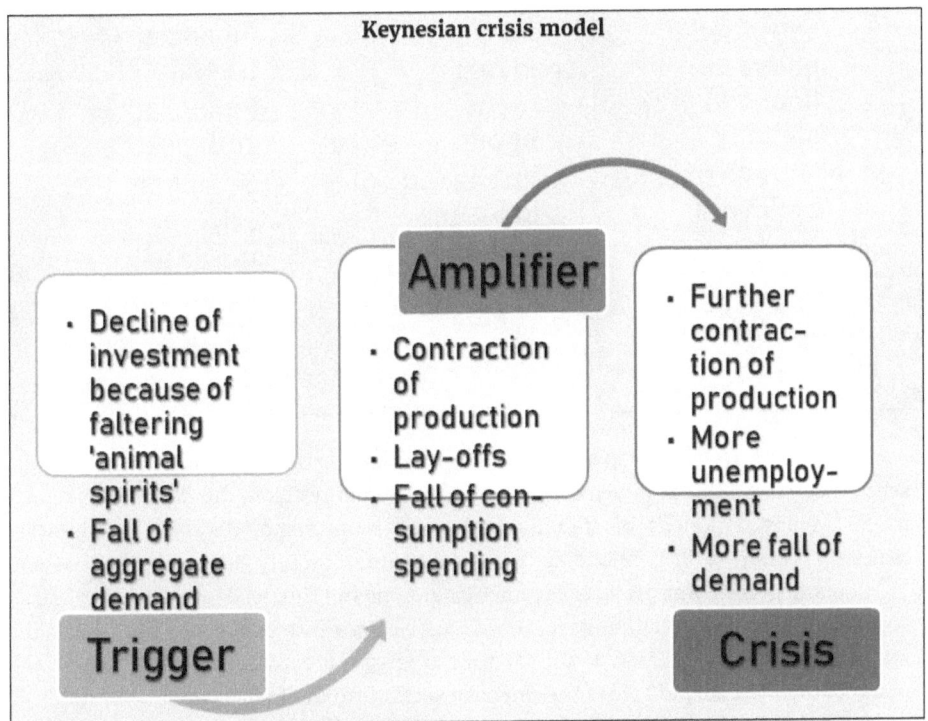

The Keynesian economic theory suffers from the omission that it does not explain the origin of the fall of aggregate demand. This theory makes use of the psychological hypothesis of a breakdown of the entrepreneurial drive ('animal spirit'). The Keynesian model depicts a vicious cycle where declining investment leads to layoffs and the rising unemployment provokes a further decline in production. In the Keynesian model, there is no return to full employment other than through state intervention in the form of more government spending.

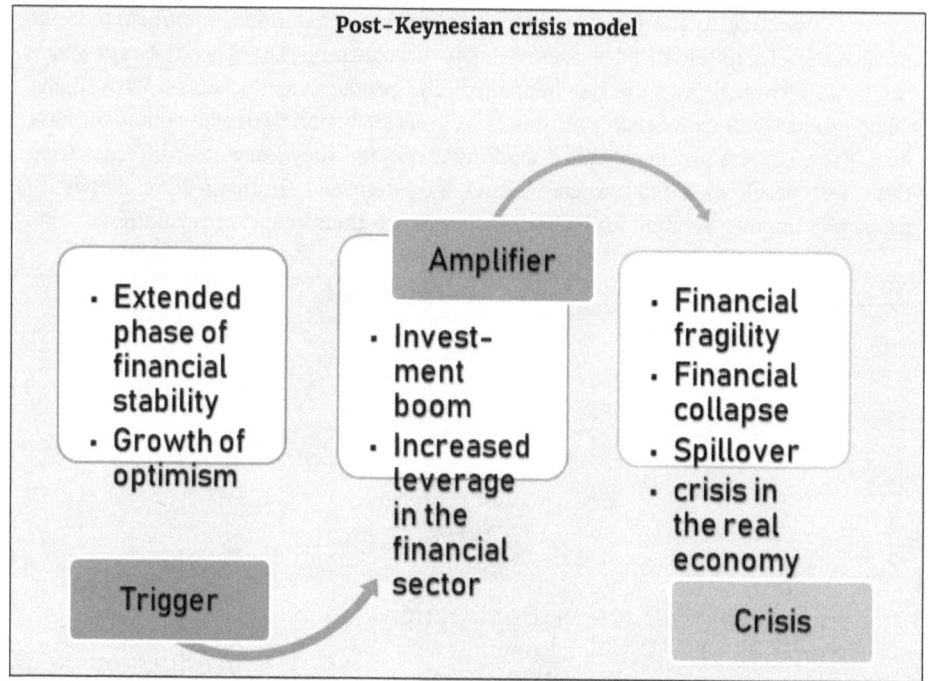

The post-Keynesian model of the economic crisis is 'endogenous' in the sense that this theory assumes that the downturn emerges from the financial system itself. Prolonged periods of stability lead to over-optimism. Rational exuberance makes it easier to get financing for investment. Stability turns into a boom. Problematic investment projects get financing. Applying financial leverage increases. Based on a narrowing capital base, more credit comes into existence. The financial system becomes fragile, and small shocks can trigger a contraction of the financial markets that will spread across the financial sector into the real economy.

The Post-Keynesian theory of the business cycle represents a poor tentative to solve the gap of Keynes' theory as to the causes of the fall of aggregate demand.

B. Exogenous Models

For the models in this group, the business cycle results from exogenous shocks. The economic actors react to these shocks, making that the economic activity speeds up or decelerates. It makes no sense to intervene in this adaptation process. Macroeconomic policy should concentrate on making the economic apparatus more flexible and take care of stabilizing the expectation, such as by a monetary policy of inflation-targeting.

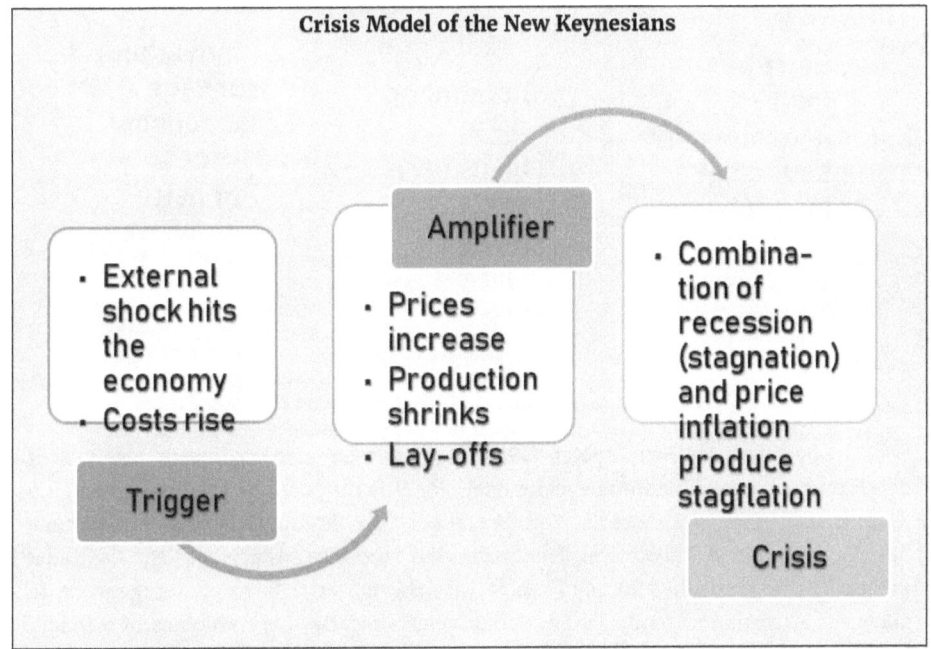

The model of New Keynesianism has been the preferred monetary policy model by the central banks since the 1980s.

The starting point of the economic cycle according to this model are positive and negative external shocks. A negative shock - such as the oil price hike of 1973 - leads to rising costs and prices and to a fall of production. The combination of stagnation and inflation push the economy into 'stagflation'.

The monetary policy rule of the New Keynesians recommends that instead of practicing fiscal policy, economic policy should focus on strengthening the supply side of the economy and increase its flexibility, particularly of the labor market. It is the purpose of monetary policy to maintain price stability and to align its measures with a pre-determined and published inflation target to stabilize expectations.

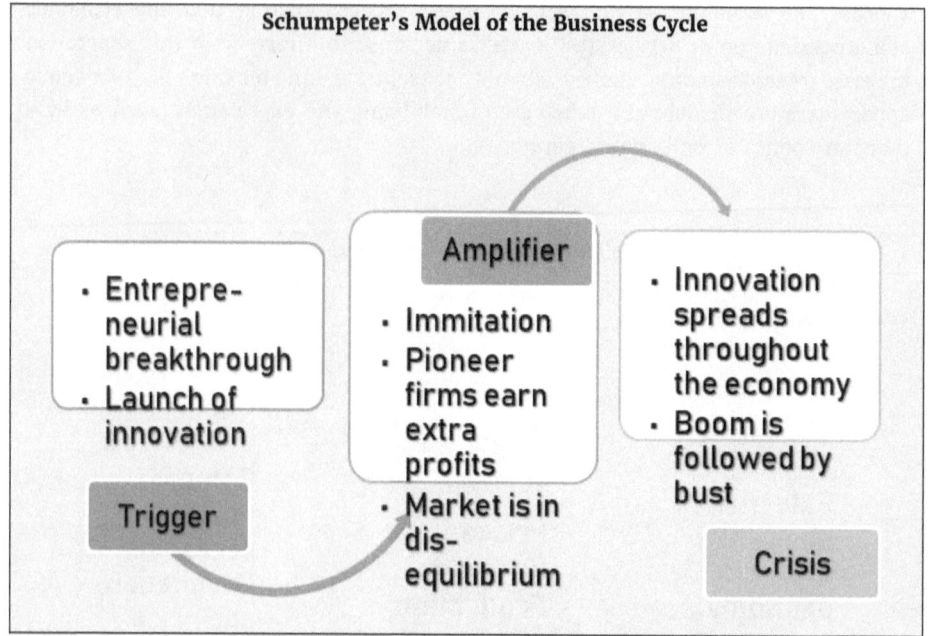

Joseph Alois Schumpeter (1883-1950) worked hard to attain his goal of developing a concise business cycle model. For this purpose, he studied to come up with a consistent framework. Yet he failed. The findings in his two-volume "Business Cycles. A Theoretical, Historical, and Statistical Analysis of the Capitalist Process", first published in 1939, show that the material is too heterogeneous to allow for a consistent model. From Schumpeter's efforts, only sketches of a theory have survived – most of it summarized in his late masterpiece 'Capitalism, Socialism, and Democracy' (first published in 1942).

According to Schumpeter, 'creative destruction' is the mark of modern capitalism and its motor is the innovative entrepreneur. Innovations disrupt existing equilibria and the innovative entrepreneur earns extra profits as long as he can hold on to a monopoly. Revolutionary innovations lead to new industries and the economy enters a long expansion.

When the innovative impetus peters out, the economy slows down, and capitalism experiences a crisis until a new cycle of innovation begins.

THE DEBACLE OF ECONOMIC STABILIZATION POLICIES

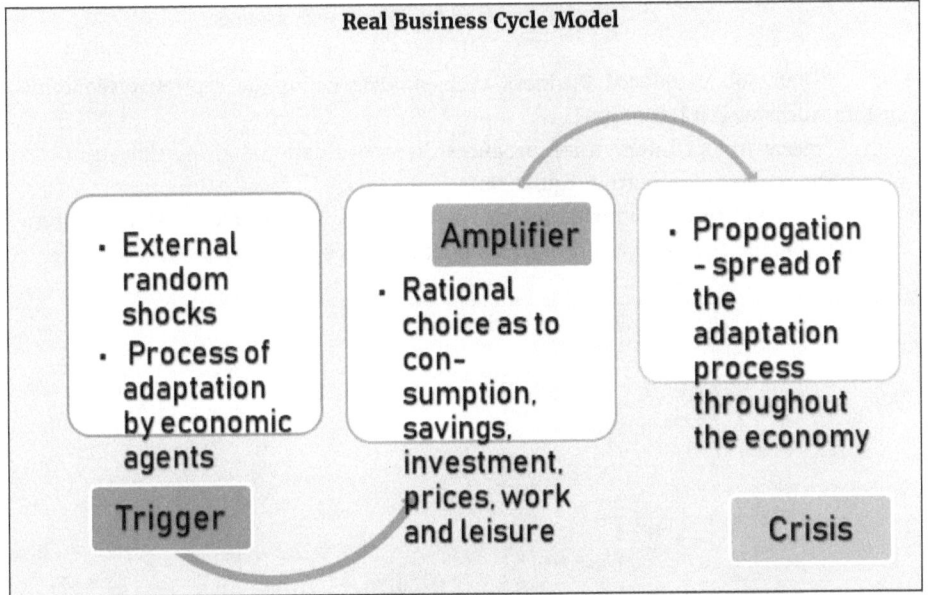

The real business cycle theory considers economic fluctuations as the result of a rational adaptation process to external shocks. The changes in macroeconomic variables, including demand and labor supply, are because of the choices of rational economic operators.

Statistical-econometric studies show that the model captures a large part of the economic fluctuations, mainly the small-scale fluctuations. The model does not explain how the major cyclical upswing and the severe economic crises occur. The Austrian theory of the economic cycle answers these questions.

C. Policy-induced business cycle models

The policy-induced business cycle models claim the capitalist economic system works well if left to itself.

Government intervention produces dis-coordination and misallocation and moves the economy away from equilibrium.

The policy recommendation of these approaches includes abstention from interventionism, to install a rule-based monetary policy, and practice Laissez-faire.

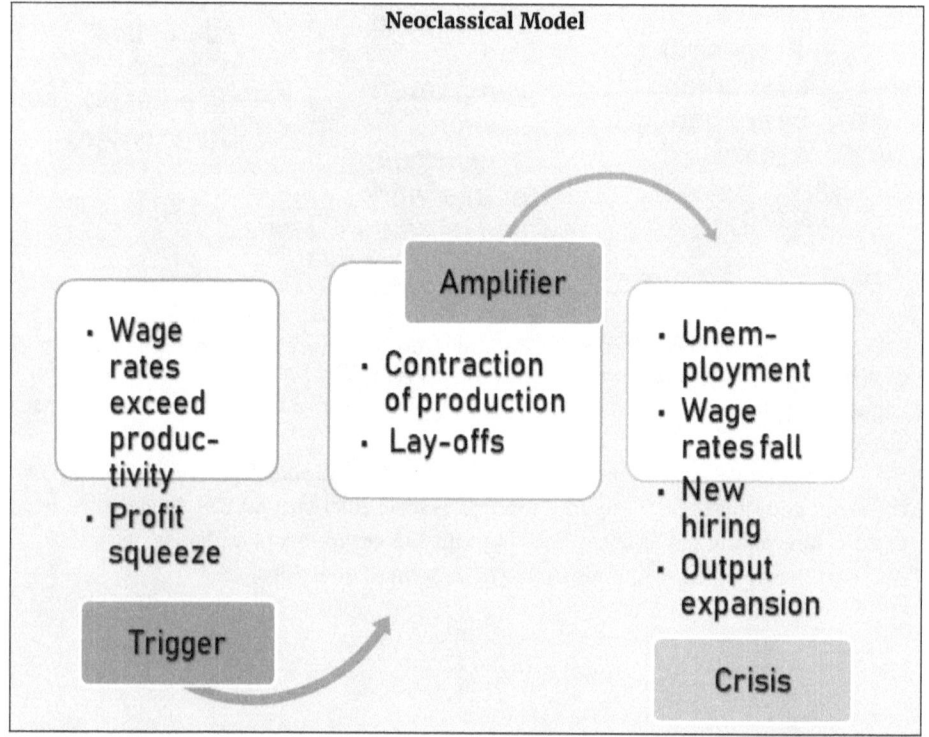

In contrast to the Keynesian model, the trigger of the crisis in the neoclassical model is well founded by economic theory.

By means of trade union power or by other types of pressure (also by the state), wage claims, which exceed the productivity level occur. Firms dismiss workers to compensate for the reduction in profits and to ward off future losses.

Increased unemployment leads to a reduction in consumption expenditures and provokes further restrictions on production, which lead to further redundancies and more unemployment and production restrictions.

In as much as wage rates adapt to the marginal productivity of labor, the economy stabilizes, and an upturn begins.

The causes of distortive wage rates include minimum wage policy, trade union power, labor laws, and other kinds of regulations such as licensing.

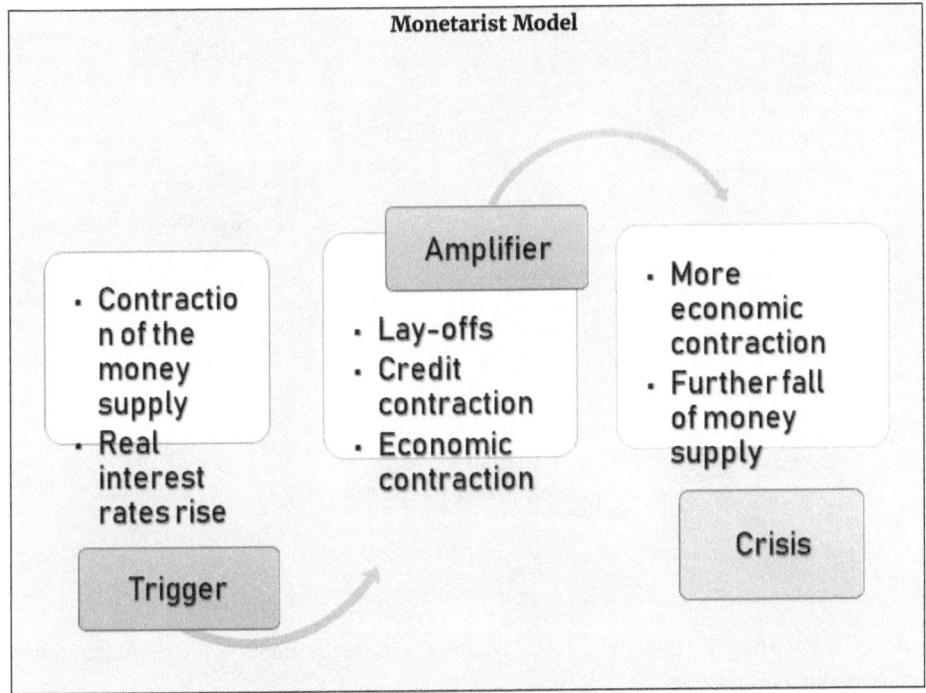

Monetarists regard money as the crucial variable of the economic cycle. The monetarist model postulates that a fall in the money supply is the trigger for an economic crisis while an expanding money supply beyond production causes price inflation. The monetarists conclude that monetary policy must take care of a stable monetary growth. They propose a constant annual increase of the money supply a little more than the rate of productivity increases. Monetarism was the leading paradigm of the central banks in the late 1970s before the New Keynesianism model replaced it.

The monetarist model postulates that an increase of the money supply beyond production causes price inflation.

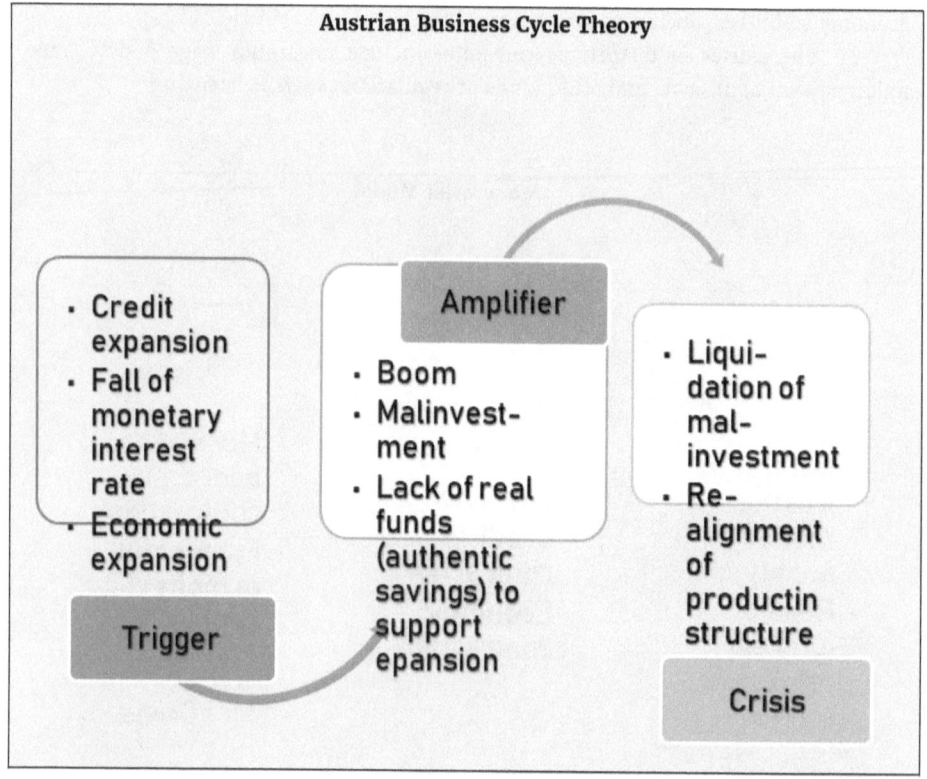

For the Austrians, the crisis comes through the boom which results from excessive credit expansion.

When the monetary interest rate falls below the natural interest rate due to a credit expansion, economic activity receives an artificial boost, and the economy overheats.

The credit expansion produces a false boom when authentic savings have not risen under the prerequisites of funding the prolongation of the investment projects. Because the new investments lack profitability, investors must abandon their projects. The economy falls into recession, and unemployment rises.

For the Austrians, the crisis is a process of healing since it leads to liquidate the unsustainable investment projects. The losses, real and potential, that come with the crisis, incentivize the efforts to adjust the existing capital arrangements and to move forward to establishing a new production structure.

The supporters of the Austrian school demand to abolish the central bank through either a return to the gold standard or by introducing private banking. There is also the model that calls for freezing the quantity of central bank money in combined with repealing the legal tender laws and thus leave the monetary system to the market forces.

The model of the 'capital-based credit cycle' represents an advanced model of the Austrian School by integrating a few of the analytical approaches from other economic theories into the Austrian model.

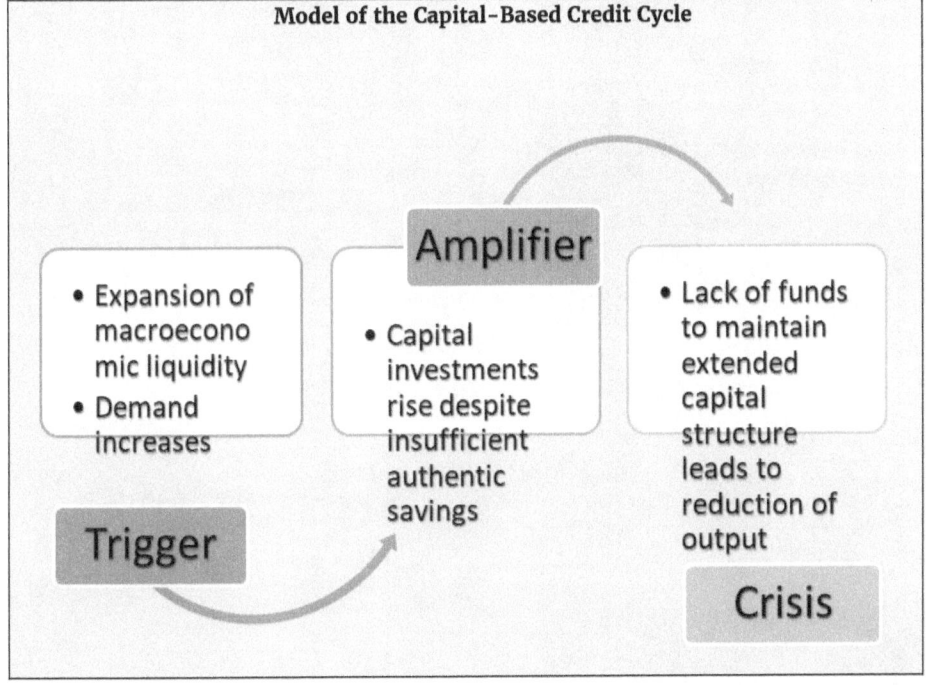

The capital-based credit cycle model rests on the equation of exchange whereby the amount of money multiplied by the velocity of circulation is identical to the product of price level and the output. Each of these two parts of the quantity equation is, in turn, identical to the nominal social product.

The large swings in economic activity (not mere fluctuations, as modeled by the theory of the real cycle) come from the macroeconomic liquidity, which comprises the product of the money base, the money multiplier, and the velocity of circulation.

The rising investment volume collides with an insufficient level of savings, which means that the investments lack economic viability.

NO CRISIS WITHOUT A BOOM

The Austrian school of economics claims both the Keynesian and the monetarist models of the Great Depression do not explain the global crises of the 1930s. According to the Austrian approach, the forced boom of the 1920s led to the Great Depression. In his book 'America's Great Depression' (1963), Murray Rothbard (1926-1995) shows how the interventionist economic policy first sped up and extended the boom and then deepened and prolonged the depression.

In contrast to the Keynesian doctrine, the Austrian school has a complete theory of the business cycle. It does not look only at the recession but sees the economic crisis as the result of the faulty economic policy of the boom. In the Austrian perspective, the full economic cycle begins not with the downturn, but with the boom.

The first phase of the cycle is the inflationary expansion triggered by expansive economic policy, with inflation lagging. A time gap opens between the economic expansion and the price inflation, which creates an illusionary Goldilocks economy where everything seems perfect for an economy that is neither too cool nor too hot. Only later, the problem becomes visible when the expansion speeds up and when it leads to a rising price level.

The second phase of the economic cycle consists in an inflationary contraction. While price inflation is on the rise, economic activity is stalling and the economy tips over into recession.

The third phase is a deflationary contraction when the debt overhang from the wrong investments becomes noticeable. The supply and the demand for loans decline; financial institutions collapse. The normal course of the economy would now be that a deflationary expansion follows the deflationary contraction in the fourth phase. Prices are falling, demand is picking up again, and the economy is recovering.

Austrians criticize that an active economic policy would prevent and delay this natural adaptation process. Economic policy lies at the origin of the crisis, and policy errors deepen and extend the crisis. When the central bank tries to fight the downturn with cheap money, it uses the same means that have caused the slump. The false economic policy stands at the start of the crisis when it produces the fake economic boom, and false economic policy is the culprit of the prolongation of the crisis when macroeconomic management tries to extend the expansion by additional monetary injections and a policy of low-interest rates.

Phases of an idealized business cycle

An expansive monetary and fiscal policy leads to speeding up the economic activity. If the stimulated demand exceeds real output, inflation will occur. The government's demand policy provokes bad investments, which provokes an inflationary boom that turns into a deflationary contraction.

If there are no interventions, a deflationary expansion follows the deflationary contraction, and the economy moves back to its growth trend. Yet when an expansive monetary and fiscal policy intervenes again, a new and stronger artificial boom follows. These cycles may go on for several rounds. With each one stimulus exacerbating the productions structure while at the surface, in terms of output and employment, it may seem that the economy is doing fine.

It is rare that governments will allow the economy to deflate. On the contrary: by policies of cheap money and higher government expenditures, the authorities attempt to stop the contraction. Such policies prolong and deepen the crisis.

In the end, the cycle will break down anyhow and leave the economy in a state that is much weaker than it would be if government intervention had never happened.

The depth of the crisis depends on the extent and duration of the false boom that preceded the bust. If the boom goes on, it is almost impossible to identify the false projects. The dimensions of the wrong investments become discernible when liquidity contracts and the funding becomes scarce. The boom ends in a credit crisis, which restrains the banks from granting new loans because they face credit losses. Investors reduce their credit demand because they fear their own solvency. In this phase, deflationary tendencies set in as overall demand falls.

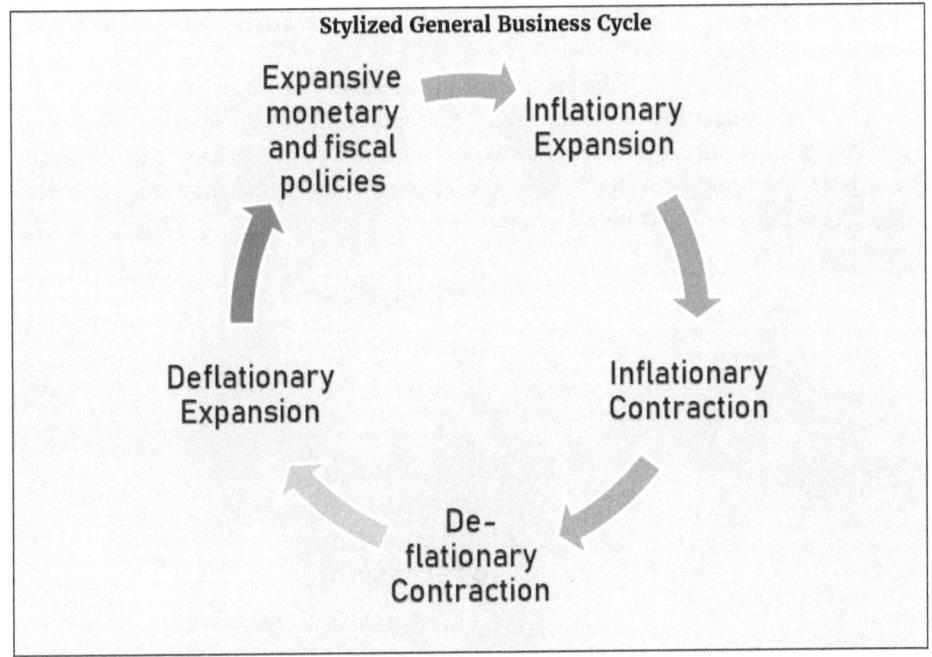

When governments and central banks try to combat deflation, they worsen the misallocation. What matters is to liquidate bad investments and not to push them further ahead with cheap money. By prolonging the boom, the economic structure suffers more distortions. As long as there is a gap between the funding needs to maintain the capital structure and the available savings volume, an expansive policy in the name of economic stability achieves the opposite effect. Instead of ending the recession, the measures prolong and deepen the downturn.

More pivotal than aggregate demand is whether information and incentives work at the micro level on the markets. This is all the easier, the more flexible and adaptable business and labor is. The more that there is a free market economy, where competition prevails, and prices result from the unhampered interplay between supply and demand on competitive markets, the fewer downturns will happen and the quicker an economy will move out from a slump if one happens. The macro problems diagnosed by Keynes have microeconomic causes. To correct the macro problems - such as mass unemployment and inflation - the causes of the problems must disappear at the level of the markets.

Strong economic fluctuations are a symptom of a lack of a well-functioning coordination in the economy. An economic policy, which does not recognize this, deepens the disorder. Instead of stabilizing the economy and to promote economic growth, the maladjustment intensifies because of the extra demand. The economy enters the vicious cycle when failed economic stimulus measures lead to more wrong economic policies.

Bad policy re-enforcement

The worse the economy gets, the more the tendency rises that the government will pursue bad policies. Wrong economic policy measures in response to a poor economic situation worsen the economy. The spiral that failed policies beget more failed policy is in full swing.

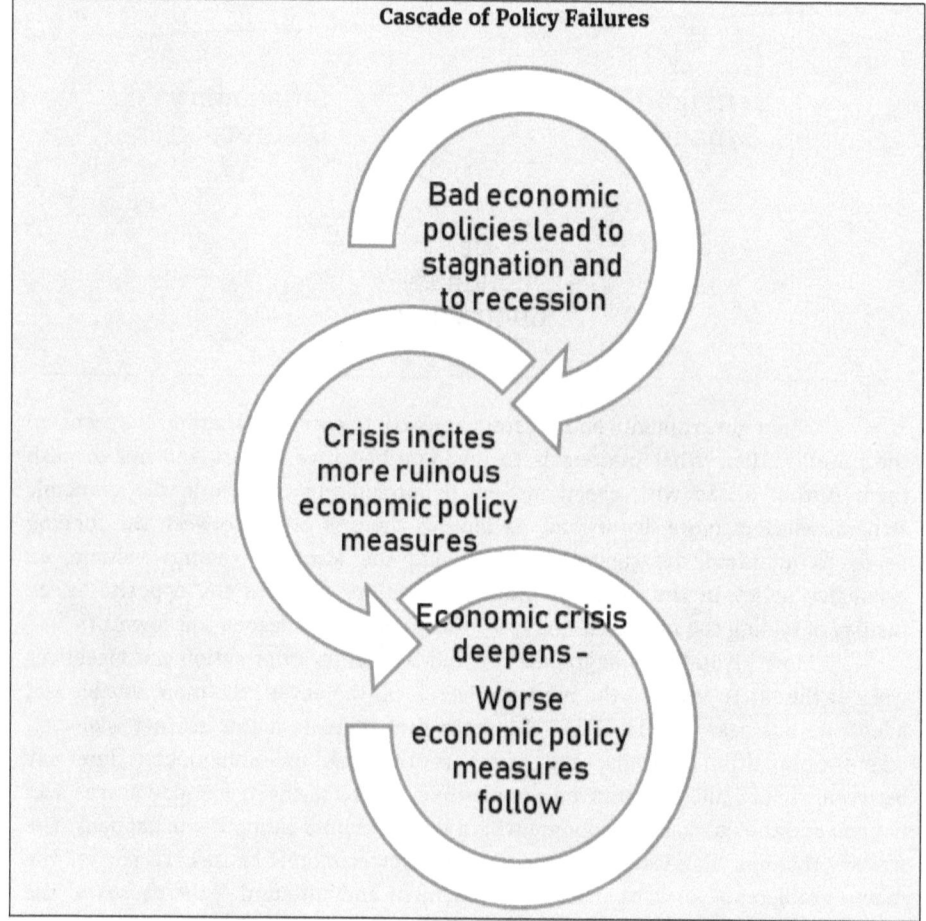

THE DEBACLE OF ECONOMIC STABILIZATION POLICIES

Once this spiral from bad to worse comes into existence, it is difficult to bring it to a halt. The economy gets out of balance and the policy, and instead of restoring the equilibrium, reinforces the imbalances. The worse the economy, the more controversial becomes the public discussion and the phonier get the proposals.

A cascade of bad economic policies leads the path to a secular decline as it has happened to many a once prosperous country. No nation is immune to this risk.

Antony P. Mueller

WHAT HAPPENED IN THE GREAT DEPRESSION?

Policy-makers claim that laissez-faire capitalism is the culprit of a depression and that an active economic policy is necessary for the economy to recover. This claim, however, does neither hold for the present nor does it explain what happened in the Great Depression. What pushed the U.S. economy into a depression was an active economic policy in the boom years and what kept the American economy so long in the slump was the active interventionist policy after the bust.

Under the presidency of President Herbert Hoover from 1929 to 1933, policy interventionism flourished. Measures designed to prevent a fall in wages hindered the natural course of a rapid economic recovery. Instead of ending the recession, Hoover's interventionism deepened the downturn. President Franklin Delano Roosevelt, who ruled from 1933 until his death in 1945, continued thereafter not only the interventionist policy of Hoover but worsened the policies. Roosevelt practiced ruthless interventionism, which included wage and price controls. He did not hesitate to preach crude anti-capitalism to gain popularity among the masses by cheap and perfidious rhetoric. In the presidential election campaign in 1932, Franklin Delano Roosevelt presented himself as the new Messiah who would save America. Yet he did not know what to do when he took over the presidency in 1933. In practice, his plan comprised pointless hyperactivity. Just doing something was more important to him than doing the right thing. One can only wonder about his policies when one considers with which audacity the government under Roosevelt violated elementary laws of the market.

Roosevelt's New Deal

THE DEBACLE OF ECONOMIC STABILIZATION POLICIES

In order to support the prices of agricultural products, for example, Roosevelt forced the pig farmers to slaughter millions of piglets. To prop-up prices for cotton, the farmers had to plow under land. Despite high unemployment, the government prevented lower wage rates. Under Roosevelt's leadership, America came under the spell of a wave of anti-capitalism, and a wild rhetoric damned entrepreneurs and bankers by blaming them for the depression. Roosevelt established a network of informants who monitored prices and wages and spied on the American population. The Great Depression happened not because of the free market economy and it lasted so long because of state interventions. Not a savage capitalism caused the great crisis, but the duration and depth of the depression resulted from government interventions that first aimed at keeping the boom going beyond its natural cycle in the 1920s and then hampered the recovery with more interventionism after the downturn in the 1930s.

New Deal policies

Year		Description
1933	EBA	Emergency Banking Act March 9 declaration of nationwide bank holiday
"	CCC	Civilian Conservation Corps
"	TVA	Tennessee Valley Authority
"	AAA	Agricultural Adjustment Administration
"	FERA	Federal Emergency Relief Administration
"	NRA	National Recovery Administration
"	FDIC	Federal Deposit Insurance Corporation
"	PWA	Public Works Administration
"	CWA	Civil Works Administration
"	FAA	Federal Aviation Administration
"	HOLC	Home Owners Loan Corporation
1934	FCC	Farm Credit Administration
	GRA	Gold Reserve Act - confiscation of private gold possessions
"	FHA	Federal Housing Administration
"	NLRB	National Labor Relations Board (Wagner Act)
"	SEC	Securities Exchange Commission
1935	NYA	National Youth Administration
"	SSA	Social Security Administration
"	FSA	Farm Security Administration
"	DRS	Drought Relief Service
"	RA	Resettlement Administration
1938	USHA	United States Housing Authority

It is not surprising that private investment remained weak under this interventionist onslaught and that the American economy did not emerge from the depression. Until the end of the Roosevelt government in 1945, the American private sector remained in paralysis because of the fear that still more encroachments on the property rights were in the making.

International aspects of the Great Depression

The 'Great Depression' was not a failure of capitalism, but the result of the First World War, the Treaty of Versailles, and the departure from international free trade.

While the tariffs restricted the free movement of goods, the international financial transfers turned into an illusory carousel. The US banks extended loans to the Europeans, particularly to Germany, to pay for the war and reparation debts, which allowed them to pay their war debts against the United States.

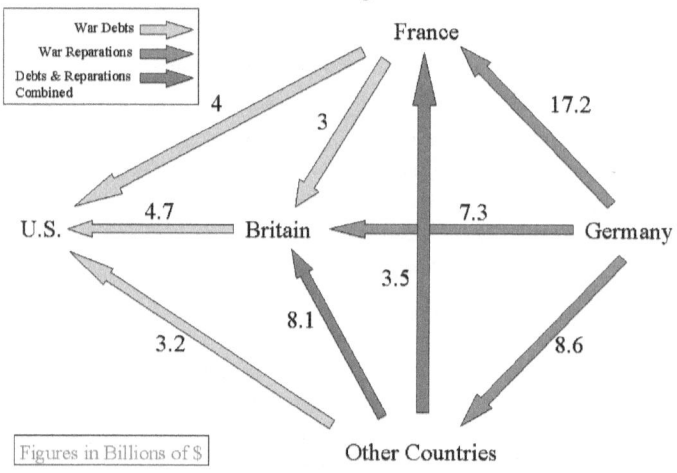

International Financial Obligations After World War I

Source:
http://spider.georgetowncollege.edu/htallant/courses/shared/dawes.gif

A fatal blow came with the Smoot Hawley Tariff Act, which increased tariffs on about 20,000 items. The carousel which got its spin from the lending spree in the 1920s turned into a contracting spiral in the 1930s.

When the protectionist measures of the 'Smoot-Hawley Tariff Act' gained legal force in on June 17, 1930, the march on the road to the catastrophe speeded up when the world trade collapsed in the following years.

The International Financial System Under the Dawes Plan and Young Plan 1924-30

Source: http://ndynes.weebly.com/the-dawes-plan-1924--the-young-plan-1929.html

As the "Kindleberger Spiral" chart shows, the protectionist measured pushed the world economy into contraction. The monthly decline in world trade from 2998 million to 992 million gold dollars based on the total world imports from January 1929 to March 1933. When the stock market crashed in October 1929, the American money lending ended, and the carousel stopped. The American financial crisis became a global economic contraction.

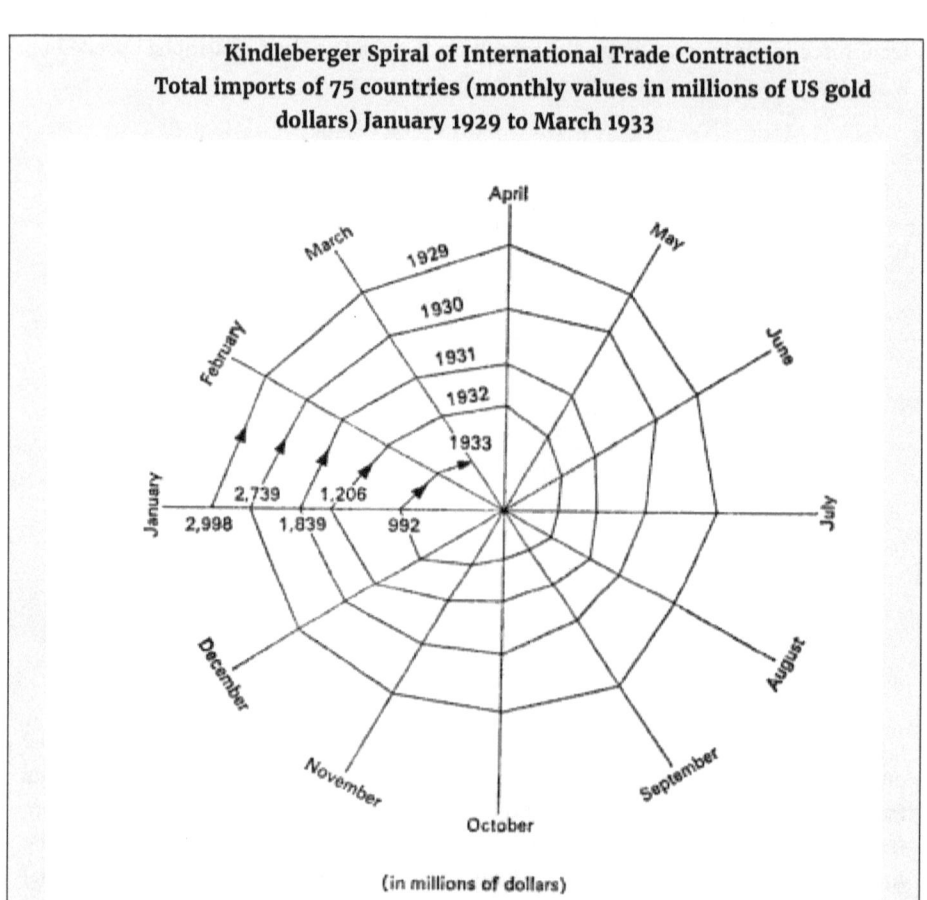

THE DEBACLE OF ECONOMIC STABILIZATION POLICIES

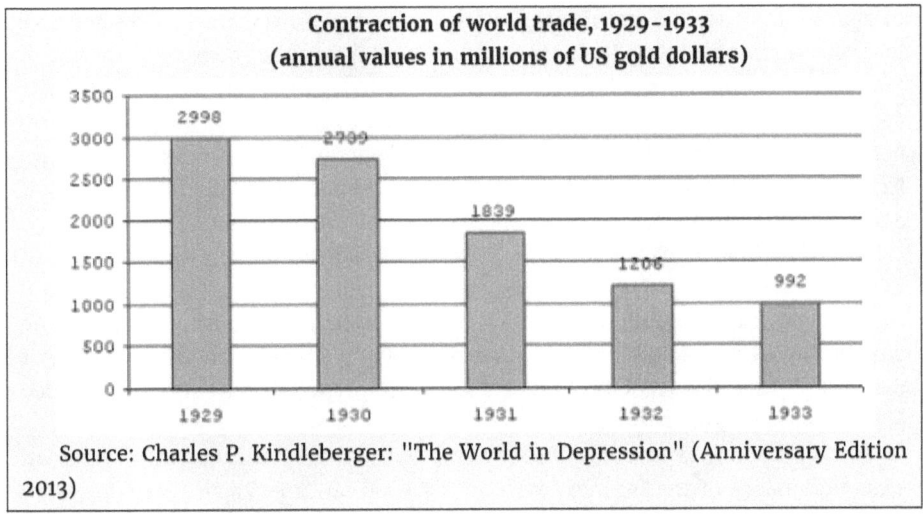

Source: Charles P. Kindleberger: "The World in Depression" (Anniversary Edition 2013)

***

The American President Franklin Delano Roosevelt has not led the country out of the depression, but his economic policy has caused that the Great Depression would last so long and run so deep. Unemployment fell only when the U.S.-government drafted millions of young men into the military service. The economic expansion in the war years came not from the economy as a productive place but in the form of a war economy.

In a full assault on capitalism, Roosevelt broke the spirit of the investors and brought down the drive of the entrepreneurs to increase production capacities, accumulate capital and maintain a well-functioning capital structure.

The capital base of the American economy eroded because capitalists refrained from providing the financial resources during the production process out of fear that the product will not receive its final payment at the end of the production line, when consumers pay, while the workers earn their wages during the time of production.

Insufficient savings illuminates the role of the capitalists to preserve the capital structure in contrast with the economic theory, which declares that economic crises result from a lack of demand. Not insufficient demand provokes the economic crisis, but excessive lending is the original cause why investors launch projects, which find no buyers as the consumers do not have the funds to pay. The problem of the crisis is not that there is a lack of effective demand, but that there are too few buyers because they can no longer afford certain goods.

A false boom begins when the excessive supply of liquidity pushes the interest rate below the natural rate. This constellation triggers a clash between the companies that will expand the capital stock and the consumers who do not save more but want to maintain their consumption level. When the goods reach the end of the production process and become final products ready for consumption, demand is deficient because consumers have already spent their funds for consumption and are unable to buy the additional amount. Then, the economy suffers from forced savings because voluntary abstention from consumption did not take place with a sufficient amount during the boom.

The low-interest rate set a false signal about the actual availability of investments. The capital structure expanded without corresponding savings. As a consequence, capital accumulation becomes a malinvestment. During the boom, no warning signal appeared because of the ample supply of credit and the low-interest rate. In the bust, the available funds are not large enough to maintain the extended production structure.

According to Murray Rothbard (1926-1995), who elaborated the Austrian economic theory of the business cycle in his book on America's Great Depression (1963), the U.S. government applied a full catalog of false economic policy measures in the 1930s. These interventionist measures explain the depth and the length of the economic catastrophe of the Great Depression. Instead of remedying the mistakes that had developed during the boom of the twenties, the Hoover government, and then Roosevelt, took a whole series of actions that had the opposite effect of correcting the wrong investment and of liberating the forces to readjust the economy.

Roosevelt's economic policy implanted measures that delayed liquidating the malinvestments. High wage rates, promoted by the support that the Roosevelt administration gave to the trade unions, led to the high unemployment. The American Presidents Hoover and Roosevelt thus exacerbated the errors of the American central bank.

Economic indicators of the Great Depression

The following data set shows that the economy did not recover with Roosevelt's New Deal but that it took until 1939 when war preparations began that gross domestic product came back to the level of 1929. Unemployment persisted throughout the decade. In 1940 the unemployment rate was still 15% - three times the rate of 1929.

After the sharp deflation until 1932, the price level rose again until 1937 after which a second deflationary phase took place in 1938 and 1939.

THE DEBACLE OF ECONOMIC STABILIZATION POLICIES

Dimension of the Great Depression
Change (in percent) of economic indicators 1929 to 1932

	USA	UK	France	Germany
Industrial production	- 46	- 23	- 24	-41
Wholesale prices	- 32	- 33	- 34	-29
Foreign trade	- 70	- 60	- 54	- 61
Unemployment	+ 607	+ 129	+ 214	+ 232

Source: Jerome Blum, Rondo Cameron, Thomas G. Barnes, The European World: A History (2nd edition, 1970) p. 885

United States. Great Depression – Data 1929-1940

Real Gross Domestic Product, 1929-1940

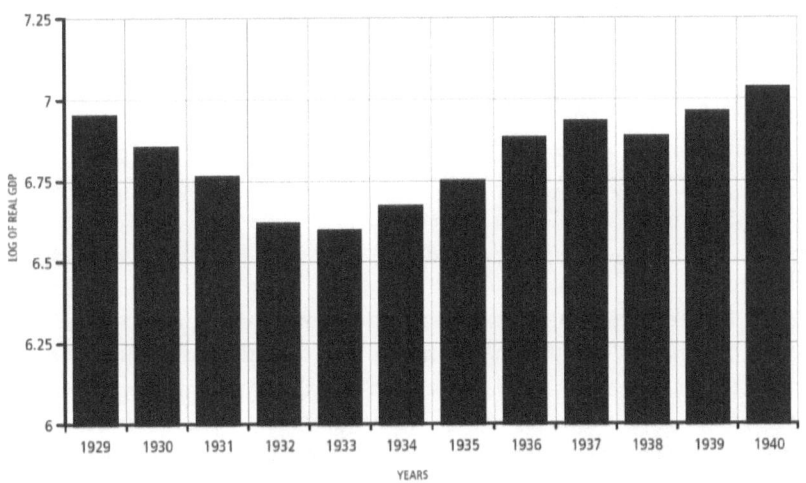

Civilian Unemployment Rate, 1929-1940

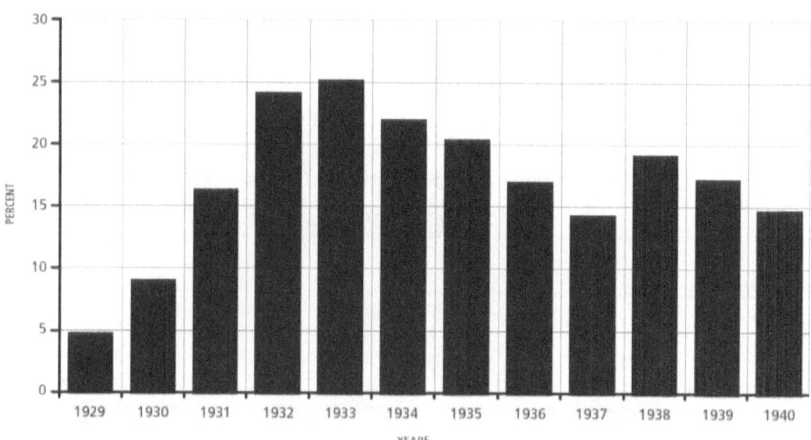

Consumer Price Index, 1929-1940

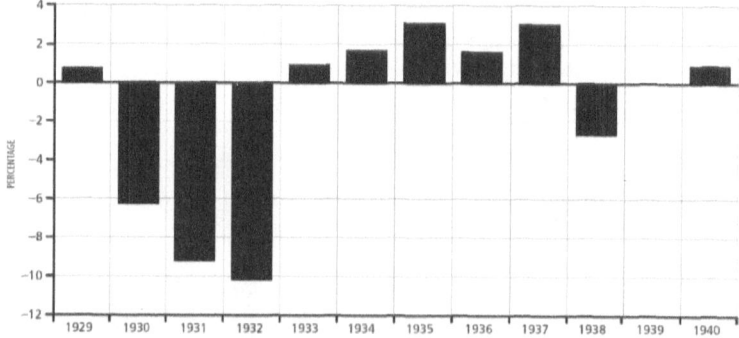

Source: St. Louis Federal Reserve Bank
https://www.stlouisfed.org/the-great-depression/curriculum/lesson-plans

Different from the United States, the recovery in Germany was swift.

The reason for that performance was that the Nazi government, which came to power in January 1933, applied dictatorial Keynesianism, which meant that it combined government spending with price and wage controls. The Nazi government could achieve this economic policy feat because it put trade union leaders and the leaders of the socialist and communist parties into preventive custody and – while keeping property rights as legal formality intact- degraded businessmen to agents of the government's central planning authority.

THE DEBACLE OF ECONOMIC STABILIZATION POLICIES

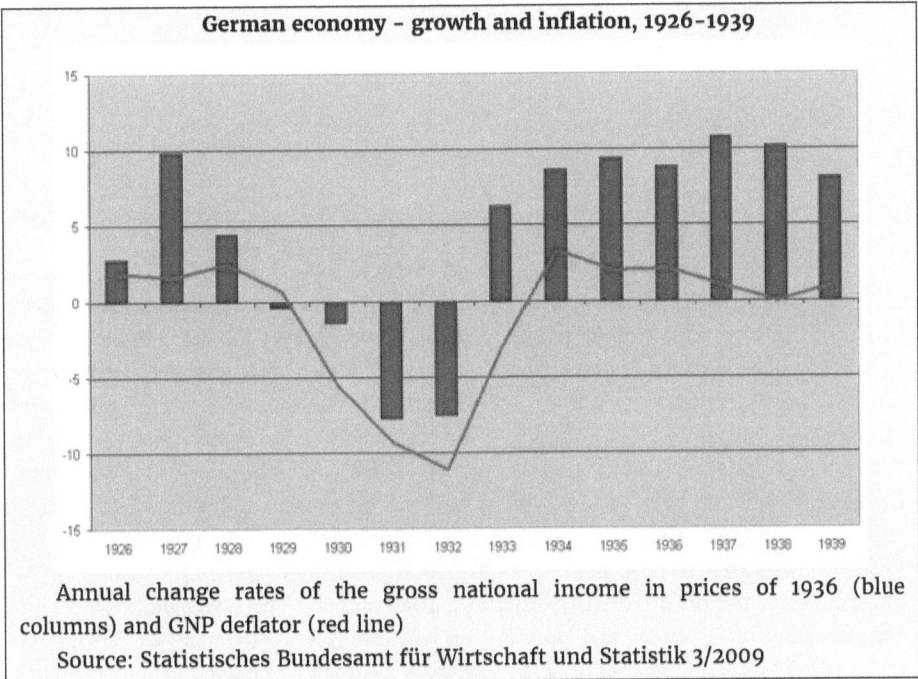

Annual change rates of the gross national income in prices of 1936 (blue columns) and GNP deflator (red line)
Source: Statistisches Bundesamt für Wirtschaft und Statistik 3/2009

A tragic element comes into play when one considers that the German economy would have also recovered without the policy measures that the Nazis applied after they took over the government. Different from what had happened in the United States, the German governments in the years from 1929 until the end of 1932 had adopted a policy of austerity and forced liquidation. When Hitler took power in January 1933, he could use the plans that laid in the desks of the former governments and start his public works program such as the nation-wide construction of autobahns. The indications are very ample that a strong recovery in Germany would have come about also without the Keynesian-style public spending program.

LESSONS TO LEARN

Governments – irrespective of their brand - like to intervene because they like to do things, which other people pay for. Governments like to combat even a small recession because it gives them reasons to launch new spending programs. The financial markets welcome any boosts of liquidity. Economic policy is interventionism. 'Stabilization' policy is the major arena of political hyper-activism. Yet these policies of stimuli undermine the economy's performance. If the state interferes with the price system by means of maximum and minimum prices, subsidies, and other assistance programs or prohibitions - and last but not least by taxation, the interest rate, money supply, and government expenditure policies – government activities distort the original market signals. There will be mistakes in the allocation of resources and competition will lose its effectiveness. Governments claim to cure the ailment that they themselves are culpable of having brought about.

Rothbard on the Great Depression

In the perspective of Austrian Economics, the recession is the phase to cure the excesses of the boom. Therefore, any attempt to postpone the cure deepens the ailment. The best government can do to promote a swift recovery is to cut taxes and to curtail public spending.

Rothbard's 'Do's and 'Don'ts' in a depression

Do:	Don't:
Accelerate liquidation of	Delay liquidation of bad investment
Let deflation run its course	Reflate the economy
Augment savings	Stimulate consumption
Reduce government spending	Increase government spending
Cut taxes	Raise taxes
Let wage rates fall	Stabilize wage rates

Source: Murray Rothbard: America's Great Depression

As Murray Rothbard showed, the governments of both Hoover and Roosevelt prolonged the Depression because they delayed getting rid of bad investment projects. Instead of speeding up the liquidation, they tried to reflate the economy, instead of letting deflation run its course, they tried to reflate the economy. They kept wage rates high instead of letting wages and prices fall.

***

The main cause of the crises in the financial and monetary markets is a national monetary and fiscal policy when they inject liquidity in excess into the economy. There is no bust without a boom, and the boom results from excessive credit expansion. The attempt to combat the contraction exacerbates the maladjustment. A new credit expansion suppresses the price signals and aggravates the imbalances. The crises deepen, and the stagnation becomes longer. The stabilization measures and the guarantees of a bailout that central banks, governments, and the international monetary organizations pronounce, undermine the risk perception of the financial market operators. Attempts to control the financial markets according to inflation targets and to reduce the private liability of the market actors promote excessive risk-taking. It comes as no surprise that markets expose abrupt, strong price fluctuations.

Regulations produce hidden costs while the so-called 'market failures' seem obvious. Thus, in a superficial populist assessment, each intervention appears as justified, whereas, in fact, regulations bring more harm than good. Each state administrative regulation suffers from the problem of the interventionist dynamics, whereupon the affected action causes side effects, which then calls for renewed control as it is also the case with economic policy.

Backgrounder: Misery Index

The so-called 'misery index' was set up in the 1960s for the two prominent economic policy objectives of a stable price-level and low unemployment. At first, this index comprised the sum of the two variables inflation rate plus unemployment rate.

Steve Hanke has expanded the original 'misery index', which Robert Barro had extended by the interest rate, with the annual rate of growth of per capita income as a percentage to deduct from the sum of the other variables.

Hanke's comprehensive 'misery index' comprises the components inflation rate plus the unemployment rate (percentage of job seekers in the labor force) plus the interest rate (long-term nominal interest rate of government bonds) minus growth (real growth of per capita income).

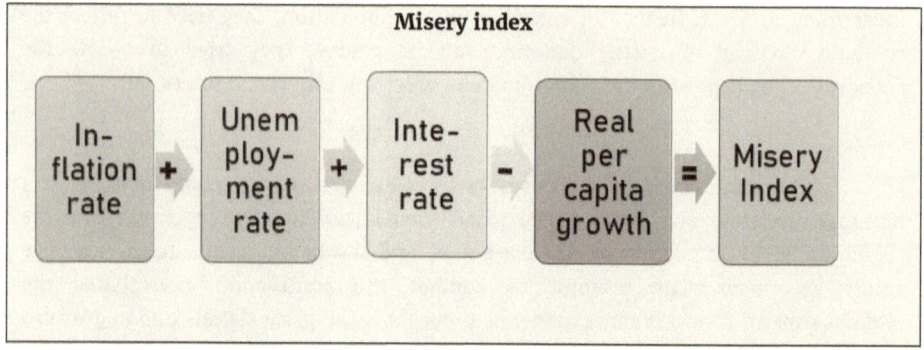

The misery index correlates with a country's overall crime rate and with the extent of corruption. The higher the misery index, the more there is criminality, and the more pronounced is the corruption. The causality goes from the latter to the first: the more corrupt a country, the higher the misery.

While more interventionism brings more corruption, there is a distinctly negative correlation between a high misery index and a high degree of freedom of the economy (according to the Heritage Economic Freedom Index). The worse the ranking of a country as to its misery index, the worse is the position of this country at the World Bank ranking of 'Doing Business', the annual survey of the extent to which governments (mainly through taxation and regulation) promote or hinder the free economic activity.

As a rule, one can say a country suffers less from macroeconomic misery the freer its economy. So why do people not choose freedom even if they could? Why do people choose their own misery? Why do democratic governments not promote the prosperity of the population but bring misery upon the people? This question leads to the theory of public choice, according to which politicians are not interested in the welfare of the people but pursue their own personal interests. For politicians, politics (sold as the public good) is not the aim but serves as a means to gain personal benefits. The politician's own well-being depends on the power which he executes. The men and women in government will gain more power by producing misery, including war, than by creating peace and prosperity. Historians do not give the title 'the Great' to the peacemakers but prefer the mass murderers. Who can blame the people for calling for the devil when they are desperate? If a politician wants to become an eminent leader of the state, he must create unrest and help create misery. This provides the opportunity that the politician can present himself as the savior of the country from the misery he himself together with his clique has produced from the beginning. So long as there is politics, as we know it, there will be no economic policy, which will serve the people. The decisive step on the way to keeping the misery index low is diminishing the role of politics and the power of the government. By abolishing politics, the state would shrink. This would make the way free for the prosperity of all and the end of misery.

***

Inflation and deflation differ from market-induced price changes if they result from monetary factors. With market-induced price changes, prices rise according to the interaction of supply and demand for this good. Prices will drop if the supply rises, and prices will rise, when demand increases, and vice versa. This is the universal law of the market. A functioning market system requires that rising and falling prices inform about the relative scarcity of a good. It is different with inflation and deflation. Here the price level rises and falls because there is more money or less money circulating in the economy. Inflation and deflation are not indicators of the relative scarcity of goods but concern the relationship between money supply and goods. Correctly defined, 'inflation' is a rising stock of money. When the money supply grows faster than the supply of goods, prices will rise.

Demand for a good comes through money. If the amount of money in an economy does not change, production corresponds to the national income. Only the relative price structure changes. Without inflation and deflation, the economic identity between the origin (production) and the use (consumption and investment) of the national product remains valid. Yet if the credit growth exceeds savings, there is additional money in the economy.

When economic actors use the excess money to demand goods and services, they will offset the relationship between the supply of the goods and their demand. Although production has not increased in line with the money in circulation, more funds are available to feed demand. There is more spending than real production. As a result, not only individual prices rise, but the price level. The relative price structure changes because the structure of production suffers from price inflation and from bad investments. Because of a monetary expansion, not only the general price level rises but also the price structure changes. Thus, a monetary inflation lays the groundwork for the next crisis.

With a proper evaluation of creditworthiness, the loan-capacity that a commercial bank grants to a company corresponds to the company's capacity of production in terms of the profit it can earn. With a consumer credit, creditworthiness depends on the debtor's ability to generate income. These factors determine the respective credit limit. This rule, however, does not apply to the loan to governments, which – at least for debt in the country's national currency – is unlimited because the state is the owner of the monetary monopoly. If the government is indebted in its own currency, it cannot go bankrupt because it can service its public debt by money creation without an end. Instead of default, which would bankrupt the state, governments opt for inflation, which bankrupts the whole country.

When there is no foreign borrowing, a government budget deficit absorbs at least a part of the savings surplus in the private sector. If the domestic savings volume is insufficient, or if the government's credit surpasses the private savings surplus, inflation will occur. The resulting loss of purchasing power of the private sector provokes forced savings later. Inflation comes into play when the demand for credit-financed demand surpasses production. Such an extra demand cannot come from the private sector because the creditors impose restrictions on the indebtedness of companies and consumers. Persistent excess credit is the privilege of governments.

The price level can also rise if the production shrinks and if the money supply remains unchanged. Here, the monetary surplus is not the result of the increased money supply, but of the relative decline in production. Hyperinflation results from two main causes – credit expansion combined with a falling production.

There are two kinds of deflation. The benign deflation results from productivity gains. It makes the products overall cheaper. If the money supply remains the same, the price level will drop. As a result, the purchasing power grows, and real wages rise. Such beneficial deflation occurs in small steps so that the economic entities can adjust their expectations and the market interest rate corresponds to the natural rate.

A malignant deflation comes from a collapse of the financial markets. When an abrupt monetary contraction happens, there is no time to adjust the terms of the standing credit relationships. Credit-related defaults will emerge along with imbalances between the amount of old debt and the current market values of the assets. A sudden shrinkage of liquidity, combined with deflation, leads to an unexpected rise in the real interest rate, which makes existing investment projects unprofitable and speeds up the close of new investments.

The over-expansion of liquidity in the financial markets precedes the collapse of the financial markets. Expansive monetary policy, which floats the financial markets with liquidity, is the real reason for the financial markets to collapse. Deflation in the sense of a monetary contraction results from the preceding expansion of the money supply. After the central banks first make the mistake of inflating the money, they aggravate the contraction in the phase of the crisis, when they try to prevent the swift adjustment of the markets to the new circumstances by renewed credit injection

THE ECONOMICS OF INFLATION AND DEFLATION

Inflation and deflation are monetary phenomena that result from the growth of money in relation to the growth of production. When monetary demand falls short of the increase of the production of goods, the price level will fall. The price level will rise when monetary demand exceeds the supply of goods.

Deflation is not malicious. Deflation is benign when it results from an excess of goods production while the money supply has remained constant. This benign deflation differs from the malignant deflation, which occurs when a monetary contraction happens while production stagnates.

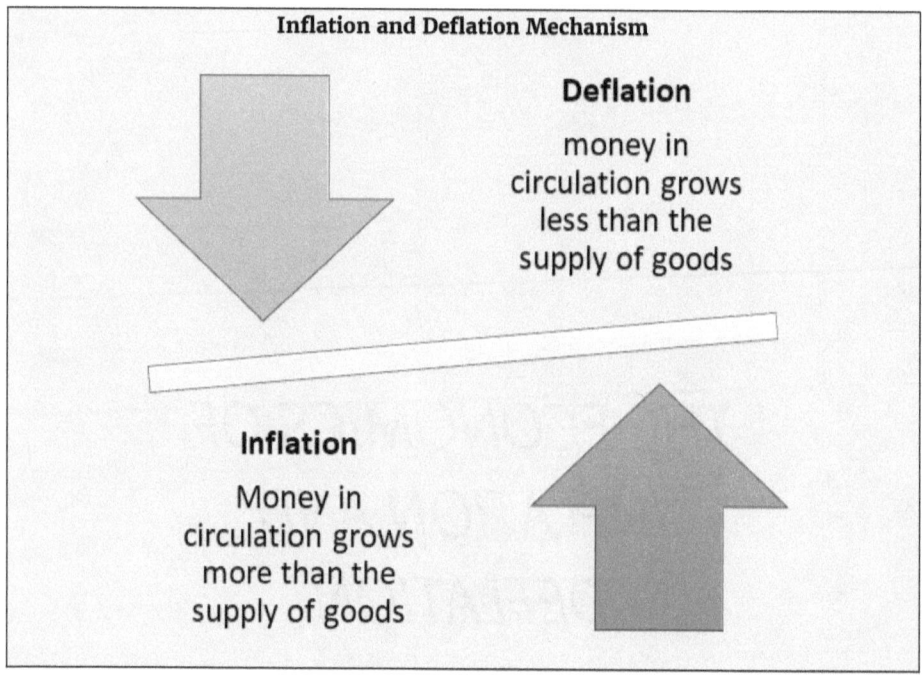

THE DEBACLE OF ECONOMIC STABILIZATION POLICIES

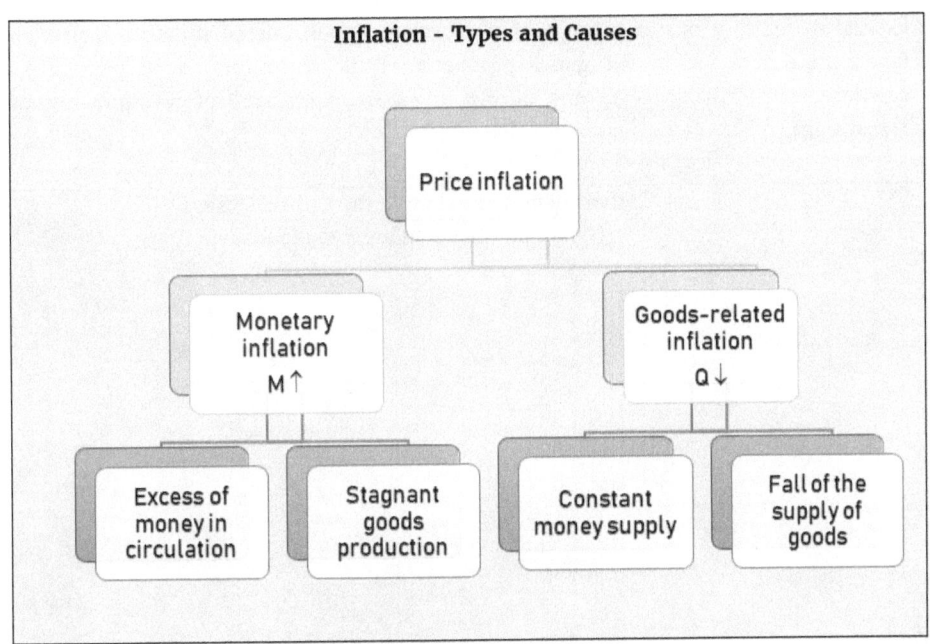

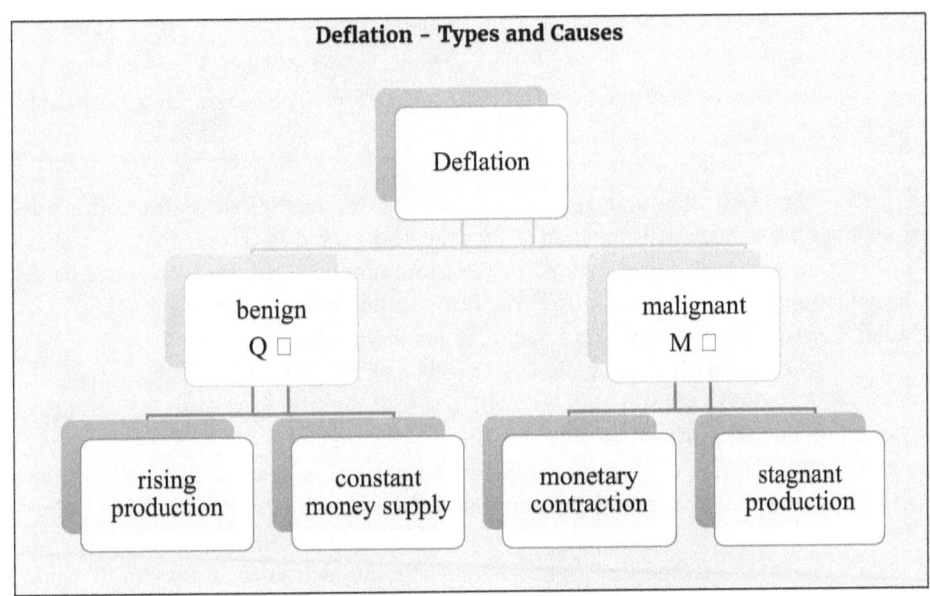

Of the two kinds of inflation, monetary price inflation occurs when an excess of liquidity meets a stagnant production. Goods-related inflation happens when there is a fall of the goods production while the money supply remains constant. This inflation happens during or in the aftermath of war and other catastrophes.

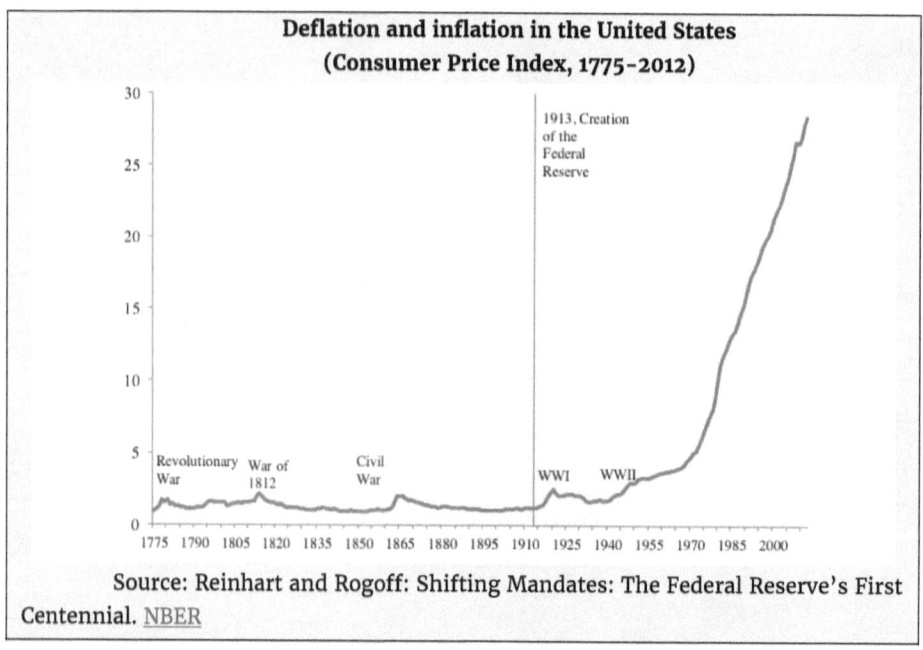

Source: Reinhart and Rogoff: Shifting Mandates: The Federal Reserve's First Centennial. NBER

The chart shows the price development in the United States using the consumer price index with the base of 1 for the year 1775. One can see that the waves of inflation and deflation remained in a narrow range before the US-central bank began its operations. The great price rises came after the inception of the US Federal Reserve System that assumed its function in January 1914.

The waves of inflation show up because of the wars: the independence war of 1775/76, the War of 1812, and the civil war 1861-65, the First (1914-18) and the Second World War (1939-1945) with the US entry in 1942.

The diagram depicts the phases of deflation after the War of 1812 until the Civil War and the 50 years of deflation after the War of Secession up to the First World War.

In 1913, the American central bank came into existence and began its work in 1914. After a period of relative stability after the end of the Second World War, a long phase of inflation started in 1970 that continues with short interruptions to this day.

As a consequence of the price inflation over the past hundred years, the U.S. dollar has lost 97 percent of its purchasing power.

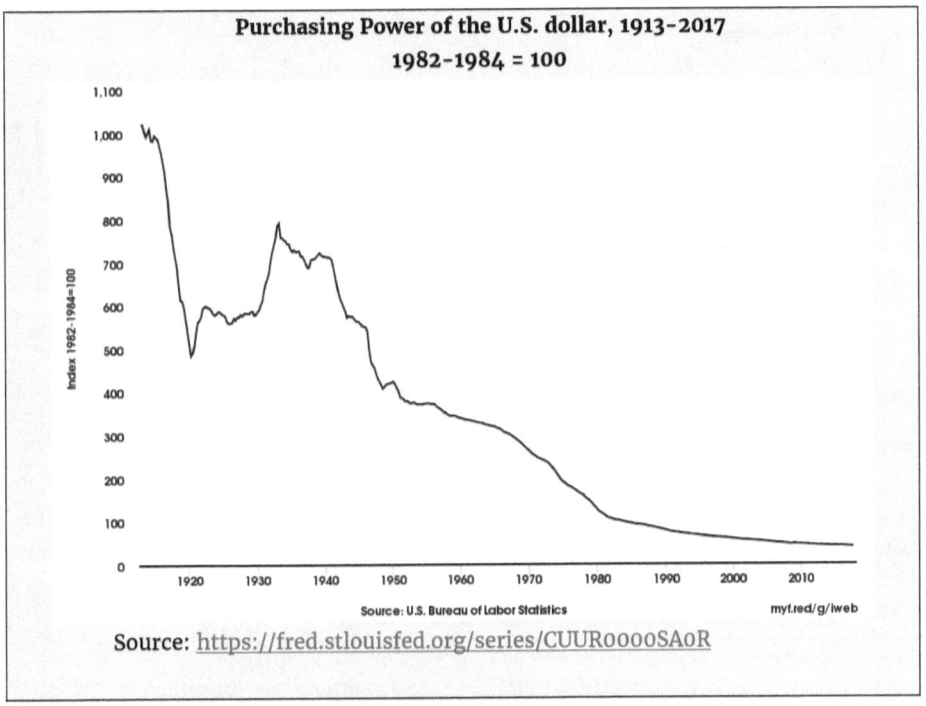

The German Hyperinflation

The German hyperinflation has its roots in the First World War when Germany left the gold standard in 1914 to finance the war expenditures through banknotes.

In 1919, there was the first inflationary burst with a subsequent temporary stabilization of the level from 1920 to 1921.

From 1921 on, the inflation rate of wholesale prices moved ahead. There was a collapse of confidence in the monetary value after the Allies presented the reparation claims to the German Reich on May 5, 1921, in the 'London Ultimatum'.

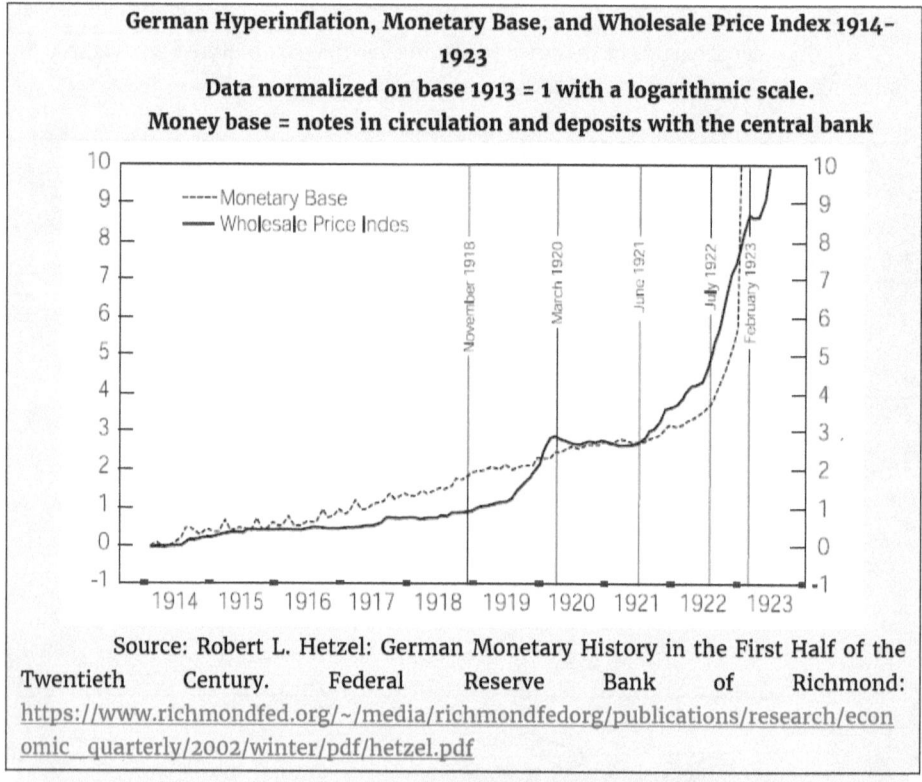

Source: Robert L. Hetzel: German Monetary History in the First Half of the Twentieth Century. Federal Reserve Bank of Richmond: https://www.richmondfed.org/~/media/richmondfedorg/publications/research/economic_quarterly/2002/winter/pdf/hetzel.pdf

In 1922/23, hyperinflation took off, after the confidence in the government's ability to service the debts accumulated during the war waned in the face of the reparation requirements of the Treaty of Versailles.

The graph above shows that until 1919, the increase in the monetary base preceded the wholesale prices. Thereafter, when the inflation expectations became more manifest, the increase in the price level precedes the money supply.

THE SORROWS OF CENTRAL BANKING

On September 30, 1979, at the depth of global stagflation, the former US central bank chairman Arthur Burns gave a speech at the meeting of the International Monetary Fund in Belgrade (at that time the capital of Yugoslavia) entitled "The Anguish of Central Banking". In his talk, Burns offered little hope for an escape from secular inflation. Current worldwide philosophical and political trends, Burns diagnosed, will continue to undermine wealth creation and curb incentives. These modern trends produce permanent budget deficits and have introduced a strong inflationary bias into the economy.

Reviewing central bank action in the 1960s and 1970s, Burns stated in his speech that '(v)iewed in the abstract, the Federal Reserve System had the power to abort the inflation at its incipient stage 15 years ago or at any later point, and it has the power to end it today. At any time within that period, it could have restricted money supply and created sufficient strains in the financial and industrial markets to terminate inflation with little delay. It did not do so because the Federal Reserve was itself caught up in the philosophic and political currents that were transforming American life and culture'.

It is the same in other parts of the world where almost all the modern central banks are functioning in a similar political environment and thus behave in the same fashion leading to the 'anguish of central banking'.

Central banks are not only hostages of their political environment, but they are also technically and intellectually not up to their job. Central bankers make errors and encounter surprises at practically every stage of the process of making monetary policy; misinterpretations of statistics abound, and there is also no reliable scientific guide for central banking: 'Monetary theory is a controversial area. It does not provide central bankers with decision rules that are at once firm and dependable'.

Burns ended his speech by saying: 'My conclusion that it is illusory to expect central banks to put an end to the inflation that now afflicts the industrial democracies does not mean that central banks are incapable of stabilizing actions; it simply means that their practical capacity for curbing an inflation that is continually driven by political forces is very limited'. Central bankers still meet surprises 'at practically every stage' of the process of making monetary policy, and modern interventionist academic monetary theory has contributed very little 'to provide central bankers with decision rules that are at once firm and dependable'.

What has changed since then? Are central banks up to their job by now? Have they learned how to interpret statistics correctly? Have they gained true independence? A superficial answer may say yes: Paul Volcker came in, put on the brakes, wiped out inflationary expectations, and opened the door to decades of stability. And then came Alan Greenspan to carry on and brought modern central banking to its epitome.

In a more realistic assessment, however, the answer must be that not much has changed. Inflation seems to be more benign nowadays, but it is a harsh twist of words to say that there is price stability when, since 1980, the official price index has more than doubled.

THE DEBACLE OF ECONOMIC STABILIZATION POLICIES

While the 1950s saw a phase of relative stability, the United States entered a long inflationary phase. In the late 1960s and experienced an inflationary surge in the late 1970s. Since 1980, the U.S. consumer price index has more than doubled from 100 to around 250 index points in 2017.

***

Seen in a long-term historical perspective, we still live in an inflationary age, and the turning point for the United States can be nailed down as the year 1914 when the US central bank began its operations. It took only a few years for the Federal Reserve System to create an inflationary boom ushering the way to the Great Depression later. The 'stability' of the 1930s and 1940s came about with the Great Depression and the price controls during the war. After that episode, prices began their steady rise, first slowly, then, since the late 1960s, more sped up. In a long-term perspective, the slowing of the price increases in the 1980s and 1990s is nothing more than a slight flattening of the curve.

Since abandoning the gold standard, we entrust two of the central prices in the economy—the interest rate and the exchange rate—to governmental bureaucrats for them to manipulate. Presumably, they know what they are doing, and they are doing it for the best of the country. Facts speak against this presumption.

After a short period of curbing the money supply in 1979 and 1980—more by accident in its impact than by deliberate design—the US central bank has turned again into a debt creation machine that inundates households, companies, government and the globe with dollars. Foreign central banks and governments are eager to join in, each of them pursuing to gain a temporary advantage by targeting the United States as the willing absorber of exports. What is going on now is global debt creation at an unprecedented pace, and the major players in this game are central banks under the obvious or implicit tutelage of their governments.

**Global Money Creation by the Major Central Banks
Policy of Quantitative Easing (since 2008)**

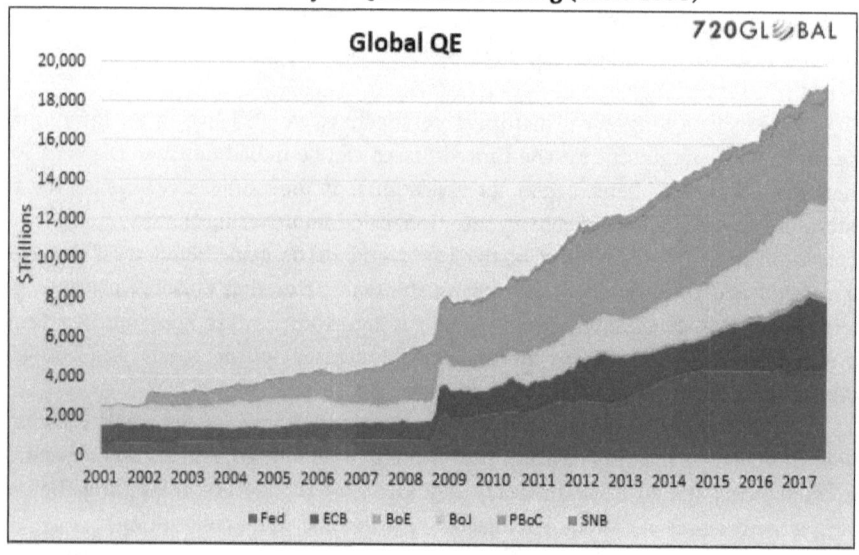

Source: https://www.etftrends.com/end-qe-means-higher-rates-resilient-stock-markets-and-higher-volatility/

THE DEBACLE OF ECONOMIC STABILIZATION POLICIES

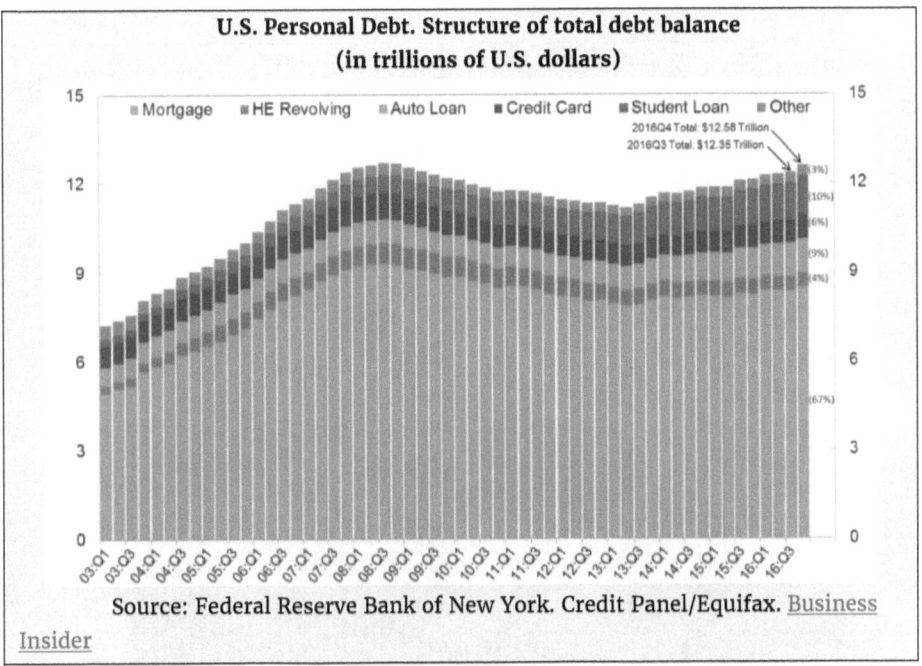

Source: Federal Reserve Bank of New York. Credit Panel/Equifax. Business Insider

The total debt balance of U.S. individuals amounted to 12.6 trillion U.S. dollar at the end of 2016. While the largest parts, which comprises mortgage debt, student and auto loans have been growing.

Driven by the relentless creation of liquidity by the central banks, global debt has reached exorbitant heights.

Global debt rose to $237 trillion in the fourth quarter of 2017 and achieved a ratio of debt-to-gross domestic product 317.8 percent of GDP.

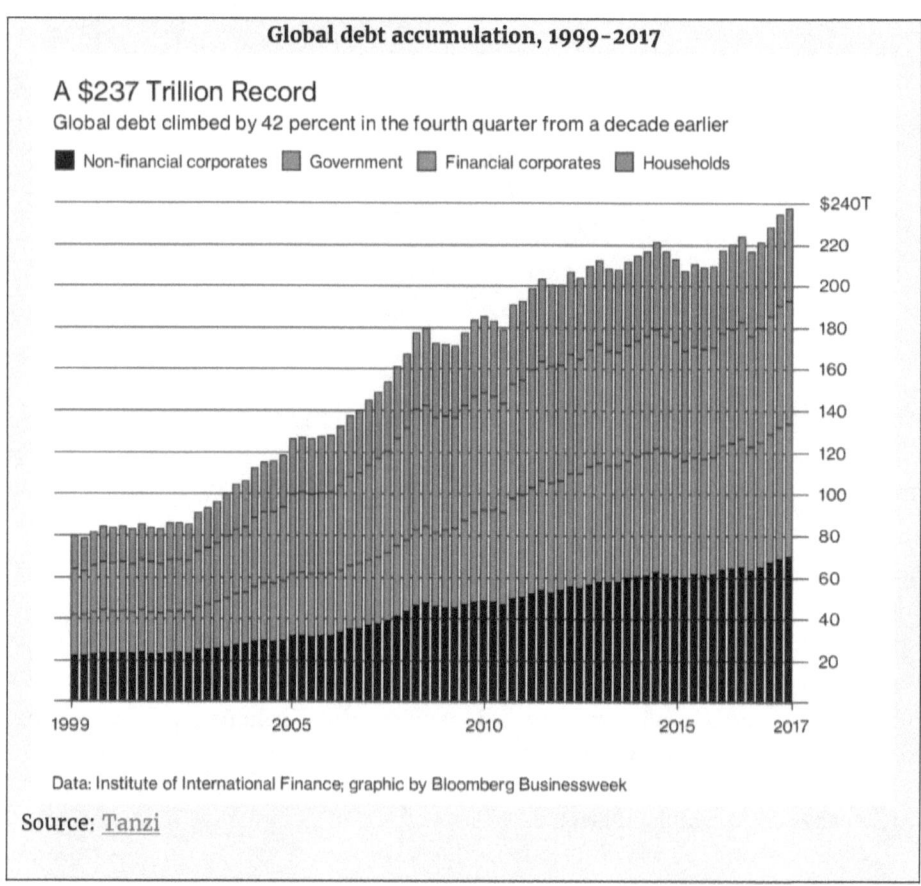

Registered inflation rates have been more subdued since the 1980s, but inflation is not 'dead', and the inflationary age has not yet ended, and it will not end as long as central banks and governments hold the lever to create money more or less at will. No less so when Burns practiced central banking, the interventionist policies of today's central banks lack a reliable basis in monetary theory, diagnostic errors abound, and the inherent inflationary bias of central banks is still alive. While until 2018 inflation was still benign, it may turn malicious again.

It seems an idle game to expect better central bankers or improved analytical tools or—for heaven's sake—more reliable econometric models. The right way to look for the escape is moving toward different institutional settings like that envisioned by Friedrich Hayek under the heading of a 'denationalization of money', by which it is suggested to dissolve the monopolistic structure that characterizes modern central banking.

Ludwig von Mises in "Human Action" put the problem this way: "Credit expansion is the government's foremost tool in their struggle against the market economy. In their hands it is the magic wand designed to conjure away the scarcity of capital goods, to lower the rate of interest or to abolish it altogether, to finance lavish government spending, to expropriate the capitalists, to contrive everlasting booms, and to make everybody prosperous"—with the consequence that such an artificial boom will lead to the bust.

Modern central banks will, at best, do little other than to 'undernourish' the trend towards inflation—when they are good at their job and helped by some luck. Faced with the choice between putting a serious strain on the financial markets and industry to end inflation or letting the boom go on beyond control, they will opt for the latter. In the current institutional setting, it is the natural tendency of central banks to produce unsustainable booms first and prolong the inevitable slump in the aftermath.

Antony P. Mueller

INFLATION-TARGETING

A central bank that pursues an inflation-targeting monetary policy model would raise the policy interest rate (which in the case of the United States is the federal-funds rate) when the current price-inflation rate moves beyond the target. The central bank will reduce the policy interest rate when the inflation rate falls below the predetermined range. Operationally, the inflation rate is the target variable of this approach while the policy interest rate serves as the instrument variable. Different from monetarism, the monetary aggregates play only a secondary or no role at all in the inflation-targeting model.

Inflation targeting is not new. Its basic idea comes from the American economist Irving Fisher (1867–1947). The Fed implemented a rudimentary form of inflation targeting after it became operative in 1914 and practiced a policy of 'stabilizing the price level' in the 1920s, in the decade before the Great Depression.

The 1920s marked a period of rapid accumulation of debt that until 1929 came along with a rise in financial wealth due to a stock-market and a housing boom. The collapse of the stock market, which began on Thursday, October 24, 1929, ushered the American economy into the Great Depression, which lasted over a decade.

During the 1920s, the US monetary authorities were not much concerned with credit expansion because the focus was the 'price level' — a statistical construct that Irving Fisher had promoted. Noticing that the price level was 'stable', the Federal Reserve felt no need to change its course or to become preoccupied with what was going on. The Roaring Twenties were, in fact, exuberant times — albeit not for agriculture. Manufacturing and the related sectors celebrated the new era and most of all this decade was one more heyday for Wall Street after the financial bonanza that World War I had delivered as the great enrichment of the United States.

The focus on price inflation had induced the monetary authorities to ignore credit growth and monetary growth as well as to disregard the productivity gains of the US economy in this period. The Fed felt vindicated for letting the monetary aggregates expand because the price level remained stable. The monetary authorities paid no consideration to the notion that with productivity advances, the price level should fall as it had been when the United States was still on a full gold standard, and thus the quantity of money was constant. In the 1920s, with an almost exclusive focus on the price level, the American central bank did not hold the quantity of money constant, which would have meant deflation, but allowed expanding the money supply because there seemed to be no reason to worry if the price level stayed stable.

When the decline of the price level results from productivity gains, the fall of prices represents a benign deflation, and the central bank should not fight it. When it does, its monetary policy is de facto inflationary albeit prices do not rise. Inflation, correctly defined, means monetary expansion, and this took place in the 1920s.

The boom of the 1920s

From 1919 to 1929, the U.S. economy experienced a period of tremendous productivity gains, both for labor and capital.

United States. Labor and capital productivity, 1899-1937

Period	Labor Productivity	Capital Poductivity
1899-1909	1.30	- 1.62
1909-1919	1.14	- 1.95
1919-1929	5.44	4.21
1929-1937	1.95	2.38

Average Annual Rates (%) of Labor and Capital Productivity Growth, 1899-1937
Source: Devine, Warren D., Jr. "From Shafts to Wires: Historical Perspectives on Electrification." The Journal of Economic History 43 (1983): 347-372, Table 3
https://eh.net/encyclopedia/the-u-s-economy-in-the-1920s/

While in the decade before, labor productivity rose 1.14 percent per year and in the 1930s the rate was 1.95 percent, it amounted to 5.44 in the 1920s. These high rates of labor productivity gains came with amazing rates for capital productivity, which rose by an annual rate of 4.21 from 1919 to 1929.

During the Great American Boom that took off after the recession of 1921, the consumer price index remained stable, rising until 1926 and then falling until the outbreak of the Great Depression, which from the 1930s onwards experienced a malignant deflation. By not letting a benign deflation happen in the 1920s, the U.S.-American central bank provoked a malicious deflation in the 1930s.

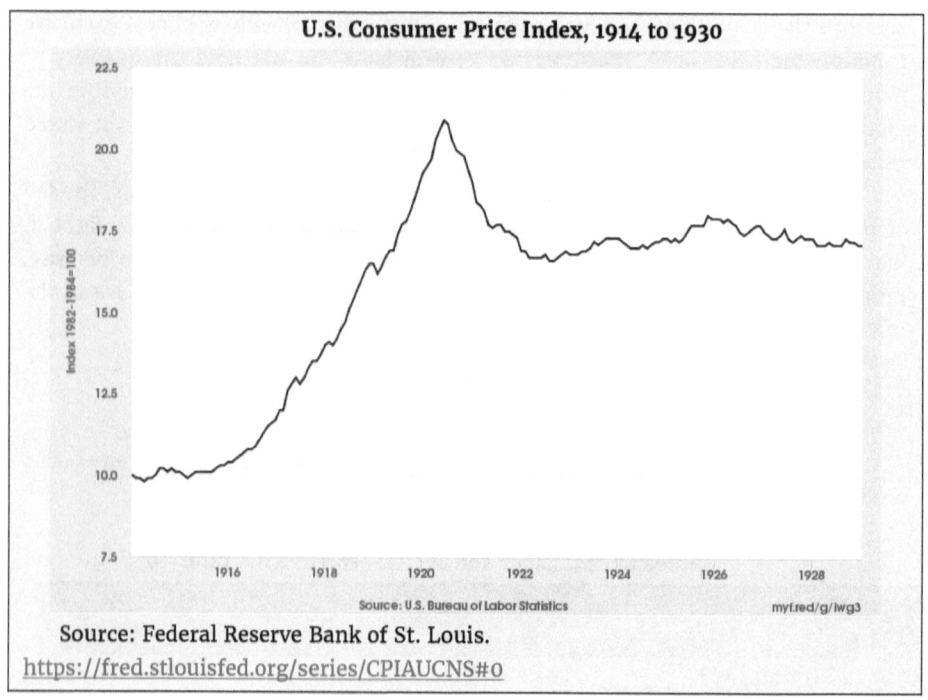

Source: Federal Reserve Bank of St. Louis.
https://fred.stlouisfed.org/series/CPIAUCNS#0

In the years before the onset of the Great Depression, there was a massive increase of bank lending from 1923 to 1929, which did not concern the members of the policy-making committee of the Federal Reserve System because they deemed that everything was O.K. as long as the price level remained 'stable'.

According to data of the Federal Reserve System, U.S. bank lending rose from seven billion in 1923 to almost ten billion US dollars in 1929 from where it collapsed during the Great Depression to around five billion US dollars from 1933 to 1936.

What had happened in the 1920s was a wrong response of the monetary policy-makers to the widening divergence between the agricultural and industrial sector of the U.S.-economy. While agriculture fell into depression already after World

War I, US industry experienced a monetary-induced boom. On average, the price level appeared steady, although its stability resulted from a leveling out due to a deflationary depression of the agriculture sector and an inflationary boom of the industrial sector. Particularly in phases when the unemployment rate was above the acceptable level, low rates of the consumer price index have served as a justification to bring down interest rates to low levels. In many parts of the world where monetary policy uses an inflation-targeting framework, it has become a rule to ignore the growth of the monetary aggregates and bringing down the interest rate. Inflation targeting has led monetary authorities to ignore not only money and credit growth but also asset prices along with other variables such as the exchange rate.

The latest episode of a mega boom occurred in the 1990s when, as in the 1920s, there was a stock-market bubble combined with a massive increase of indebtedness of consumers for housing and consumption goods. Central bankers did not pay much attention to the money supply and remained sanguine throughout the period that led up to the crisis of 2008. The mantra of monetary policy was that if the price level remained stable and with only moderate price inflation, interest rates could fall as low as they can drop, and the money supply could grow without restraint and get as large as the demand for money seemed to warrant.

There were a series of shocks in the 1990s and in the decade before and after. Yet up to the outbreak of the crisis of 2008, one could overcome the calamities, so it seemed, by bailing out the creditors and expanding the money supply. Inflation targeting entailed a pervasive policy of bailouts and thus laid the basis of a financial culture of moral hazard.

In 2007, financial markets froze, the flow of money in the interbank market came to a sudden standstill. It was as if a cardiac infarct had hit the heart of the financial markets. Albeit shocked, monetary policy-makers showed full confidence that a proper amount of liquidity injection would make the markets move again soon; thus, they believed in their naïve conviction, the economy would recover to full bloom again. Yet doom set in when it became clear that the old recipe didn't work anymore. Despite massive injections of liquidity, markets recovered somewhat, and in 2008 a wave of defaults of financial institutions occurred. In August 2011, the United States came close to bankruptcy when Congress was reluctant to raise the statutory debt limit. Shortly thereafter, the global financial crisis deteriorated into the European sovereign-debt crisis. Greece came close to bankruptcy and contagion hit Spain, Portugal, and Italy.

By early 2012, monetary policy had reached its limits. With interest rates close to zero in the major economies of the world, it was only through gargantuan amounts of liquidity injections that the financial system got propped up. By practicing a 'zero interest rate policy' (ZIRP), by buying assets of dubious quality from financial institutions through its Troubled Assets Relief Program (TARP), and by trying to pump more liquidity into the market through its policy of 'quantitative easing' (QE), an expansion of unprecedented proportions of the Federal Reserve's balance sheet has occurred. The real or imagined assumption that the financial system is on the verge of complete collapse has brought about massive government bailouts and stimulus programs that have resulted in rising fiscal deficits and unsustainable public debt burdens. Deflation has become the ultimate scare of governments and the dreadful nightmare of central bankers.

BAILOUTS AND STIMULI

Under Alan Greenspan's rule at the Fed, the function of the central bank as a bailout institution experienced a golden age. He was the chairman of the Board of Governors of the Federal Reserve System from August 11, 1987, to January 31, 2006. Greenspan served almost two decades at the helm of the US central bank. He has left his mark like few before him.

As head of the Federal Reserve System, Alan Greenspan earned the highest esteem from the central bank's main clientele: the financial community. The adoration that the chairman received from the financial market operators and from the various governments by which he was re-appointed five times has come from the expectation he would stand ready as their bailout man.

It would be a vain endeavor to research modern mainstream economic textbooks to pin down the economic theory which guided Alan Greenspan's monetary policy. The chairman of the Board of Governors of the Federal Reserve System has let it be known that most of these models are irrelevant. The monetary school he represents is the traditional model of modern central banking. It is 'bailout economics'. It is an economic doctrine, which says whenever and for whatever reason the financial markets or the government should get into financial trouble, the central bank will bail them out by providing abundant liquidity.

As soon as the asset markets—and later the banks and the public in general—had learned about the bailout doctrine there was no stopping. Under such a cover, financial investing no longer needed prudent calculation, even more so as the chairman's visionary portraits of an imaginary world of abundance promised an oasis of prosperity on American soil. With the bailout guarantee verbally and practically in place and the vision of a new economic dawn firmly put forth, the shackles of fear that had restrained excessive debt accumulation in the past have been shed.

After the stock market crash of 1987 and Greenspan's bailout of the financial system, financial market operators have operated under a quasi-official charter, which says the central bank will protect its major actors from the risk of bankruptcy. Consequently, the reasoning emerged that when one succeeds in this game, one will reap high profits and gain market share, yet if one should lose, the authorities will save you, anyway. Under the protective shield provided by the central bank, the US financial system has become tilted toward relentless expansion. In a process that began as early as 1987, Greenspan's monetary policy has transformed the American economy toward the predominance of the financial sector and secured a bonanza for the financial market operators.

After just two months in office as Fed chairman, Greenspan set the norm when facing the stock market crash of October 19th, 1987, when he declared: 'The Federal Reserve, consistent with its responsibilities as the nation's central banker, affirmed today its readiness to serve as a source of liquidity to support the economic and financial system.'

Greenspan's prime monetary policy rule has remained the same since then. It is a rule which he formulated when referring to the response to the stock market debacle in 1987: "It wasn't a question of whether you would open up the taps or not open up the taps. It was merely how you would do it, not if.' (quoted in David B. Sicilia and Jeffrey L. Cruikshank: The Greenspan Effect. Words that Move the World's Markets. New York et al.: McGraw-Hill, 2000, p. 11)

As Greenspan explained in his testimony before the U.S. Senate Committee on Banking, Housing, and Urban Affairs, on February 2, 1988, it is the 'crucial role' of the central bank to respond to 'episodes of acute financial distress'.

The chairman has lived up to that promise. Greenspan fulfilled his mission in the wake of the 1987 stock market debacle. He made sure that the government could finance two wars in the Middle East. Alan Greenspan performed his bailout job by saving the creditors of the Long-Term Capital Management (LTCM) hedge fund in 1998, he did it in the face of an expected Y2K liquidity squeeze at the turn of the millennium, and the chairman did it by fabricating the housing bubble that led up to the financial crisis of 2008.

What Greenspan has accomplished is in line with the original intentions of the Act that established the Federal Reserve System in 1913. This legislation passed under the pretense that protecting the major players of the financial industry from default means saving the system. By making the financial system more 'elastic', governments received the prospect that from now on golden fetters no longer would curb their encroachment.

By acting as the 'lender of the last resort' to guarantee 'financial system stability', central banks implant a safety net for their debt-ridden governments and for the big players in the financial industry. With the adage of 'too big to fail', a financial institution gets a free ticket to accumulate private wealth with almost no risk. Providing unlimited money supply establishes an incentive for the governments to expand without end and for the financial intermediaries to opt for asset expansion at the cost of prudence. As bailout institutions with the promise of unlimited liquidity, it the central banks themselves that lay the groundwork for 'financial distress' to emerge—not just as 'episodes', but that makes the modern financial system fragile.

There were recessions and changes of money values before the ascendance of modern central banking, but these were short and mild and most of the time they resulted from external factors such as bad harvests and wars. With modern central banking, hyperinflations and great depressions emerged. With all anchors severed that would curb debt expansion, modern central banks create the permanent boom, but while aiming at this illusory goal, they prepare the conditions that erupt as big slumps and hyperinflations.

Modern central banks function as the prime instigators of unsustainable booms. While imposing as the navigators, they act as the prime instigators of the instability they are to fight. Greenspan has played this game in all its virtuosity. With a masterful hand, the chairman wielded the levers of monetary stimuli. He has given the financial markets what they want: a lender of the last resort that one can bank on. When one debt-driven boom had turned into a bust, he made sure that another one would begin.

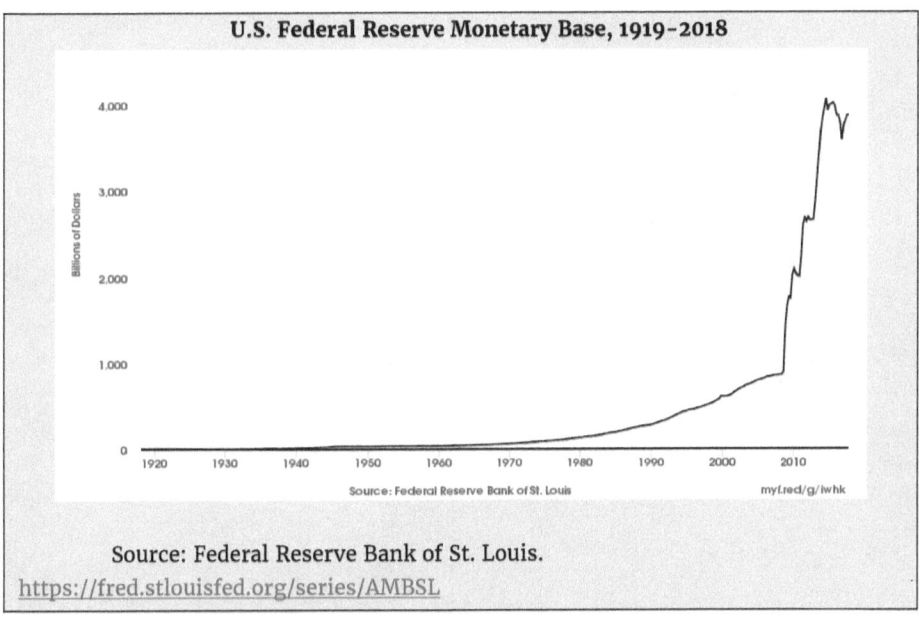

Source: Federal Reserve Bank of St. Louis.
https://fred.stlouisfed.org/series/AMBSL

The key to the power of a central bank is maintaining the illusion that fiduciary money is wealth. It is a con game, and in this respect, there can be few doubts that Alan Greenspan has been a master at this game. Under his rule, the arcane machinery of the central bank has turned into a fountain of cheap money, which has inundated the globe. This policy of repeated bailouts and providing unlimited funding for government expansion in the face of a decreasing savings rate and a shrinking productive sector is the way toward an economic Armageddon. By functioning as bailout agents, central banks use the power to create money as a power to destroy.

If one thought, however, that Alan Greenspan was peculiar in the respect, soon learned that his successor, Ben Bernanke, would open the floodgates of money even more. While under Greenspan, central bank money increased from 220 billion to 825 billion U.S.-dollars. Under the chairmanship of Ben Bernanke (chairman from 2006 to 2014), the U.S. monetary base rose from this level to over four trillion.

THE PITFALLS OF ECONOMIC POLICY-MAKING

Macroeconomic policy pursues four major policy aims: a stable price level, steady economic growth, high employment and the maintenance of the country's international payment ability.

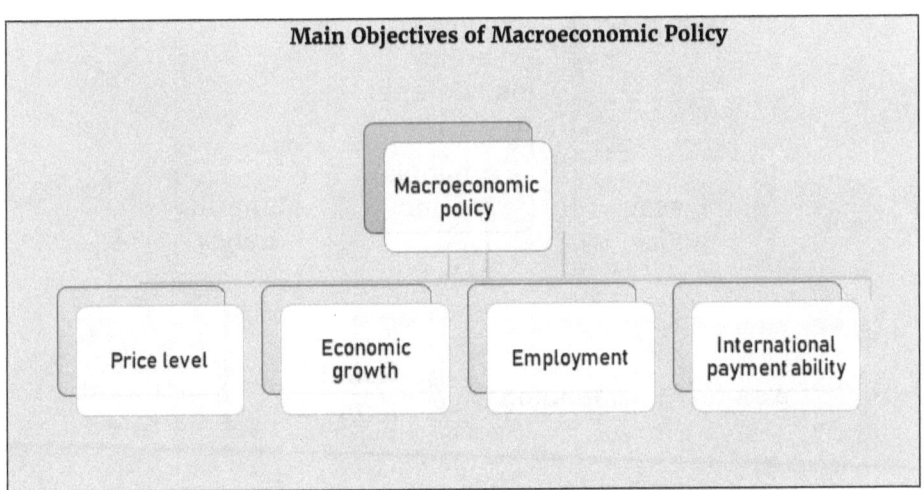

In its modern version, macroeconomic policy focuses on the price level in terms of 'inflation targeting'. By this policy, the monetary authorities announce an inflation goal such as an increase in the consumer price index of more than zero and less than two percent as it is explicitly the case with the European Central Bank (ECB). Different from the ECB, the U.S. law obliges the American central bank to include a low unemployment and low-interest rates as its goals. As spelled out by the U.S. Congress that the monetary policy should pursue 'maximum employment', 'stable prices', and 'moderate long-term interest rates', these goals are contradictory and beyond the reach of a central bank. Furthermore, Congress stipulated five areas for the central bank with mutually exclusive objectives such as conducting the nation's monetary policy, helping maintain the stability of the financial system, supervising and regulating financial institutions, fostering payment and settlement system safety and efficiency, and promoting consumer protection and community development. (see: Board of Governors of the Federal Reserve System. Purposes and Functions).

As to macroeconomic policy in the narrow sense, the policymakers have three tools at their disposal: Fiscal policy, monetary policy, and exchange rate, and trade policy (tariffs). There is a discrepancy between the complexity of the goals and the scope of the instruments. Such a construct is to fail by necessity.

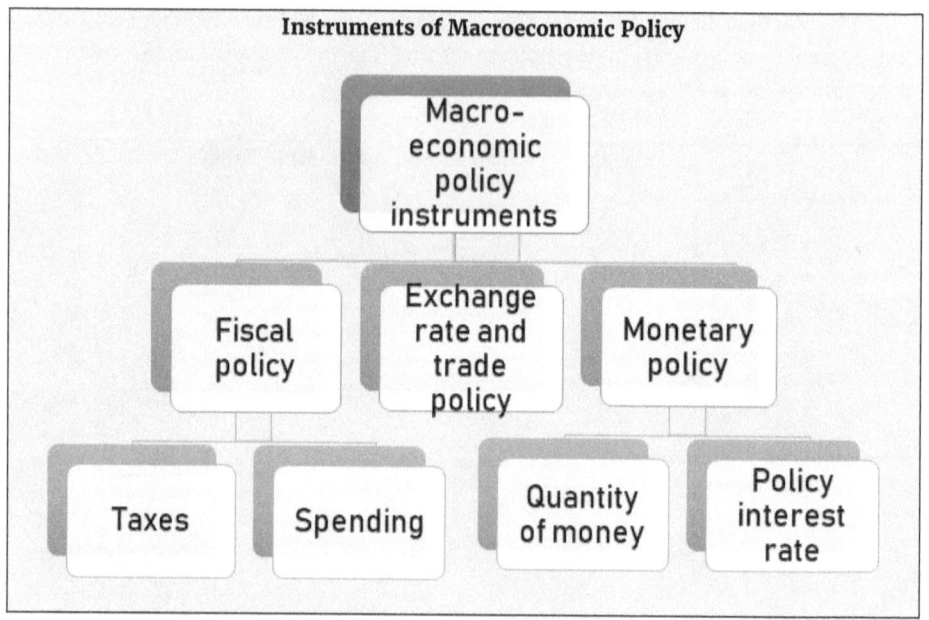

Because only a small part of government spending is discretionary, fiscal policy is useless as an effective policy instrument. On an operational level, fiscal policy plays a role only as an emergency instrument as it was the case when President George Bush launched a stimulus package of 105 billion US-dollars in February 2008, and his successor Barack Obama followed suit with an additional package of 787 billion US-dollars in February 2009.

The problem with fiscal policy is that debt-financed expenditures increase public debt and therefore the effect will backfire. Tax policy is too cumbersome as an effective policy instrument. This leaves macroeconomic policy with only monetary policy. While monetarism favored the quantity of money, the emphasis has shifted back to interest rate policy after the problems of practical monetarism became apparent.

John Taylor (1946*), while working at the U.S. Treasury in the early 1990s, has captured this shift in a formula which became popular as the so-called 'Taylor Rule'. This rule assumes that the monetary policy follows an explicit inflation target and that the long-run real growth rate of the economy follows a natural path that is determined by factors outside of the control of the monetary policy – such as capital accumulation, education, and innovation. Taylor also postulates a natural real rate of interest. The formula stipulates quantitatively by how much the policy interest rate must change when the actual inflation rate deviates from the target rate and the actual economic performance deviates from the economy's potential. The modified Taylor Rule substitutes the natural unemployment rate for the indicator of the capacity utilization.

Things get complicated when international economic aspects come into play. The interest rate is not neutral as to the exchange rate and the exchange rate affects the price of imports and exports and feeds back on the price level and on the import and export sectors of the economy.

Even this cursory glance at the intricacies of economic policy should reveal that managing the economy is a mission impossible. Any ambition of improving economic policy to make it more effective will fail. The path to go is not the technical improvement but to abandon policy altogether and let the markets do the job. Not the vile attempt to improve economic policy is the way but less intervention. Instead of more activism, economic policy should find ways to promote such institutions that foster the autoregulation of the markets. The freer the markets, the less market intervention, the better is the economic performance and the less there is the need for economic policy.

It is time for a change. Instead of more policy intervention there should be less. In accordance with the shift to anarcho-capitalism and demarchy, a new matrix for economic policy must take shape in the process of moving to a stateless society.

Economic Policy Matrix of the 20th century	The New Matrix
Liberal Social Democracy	Demarchy
State Capitalism	Anarcho-Capitalism
Economic growth of GDP	Productivity
Fixed employment conditions	Flexible employment
Inflation targeting	Benign deflation
National state money	International private money
Public providers of security	Private providers of security
Public education	Private education
Public health care systems	Private health care systems
Redistribution	Minimum income policies

THE VALUE OF MONEY

There is a sharp distinction to make between the changes of the price level and of the changes in relative prices. The price level changes because of the changes of the relation between the amount of money and the volume of goods in an economy. Relative prices change because of changes in demand and supply in the market. One must distinguish between relative prices and the price level. The price level results from the relation between the amount of money and the supply of goods. In contrast, relative prices reflect demand and supply for specific goods.

If the money supply is constant, the increase of the supply of goods would bring about a benevolent deflation. Yet often the monetary authorities expand the money supply more than the economy can produce goods and the result is the general price inflation. Relative prices are indispensable to guide the behavior of consumers and investors. Price inflation is a constant risk factor for entrepreneurial decision-making because price inflation affects both the level and the structure of prices. Because the price level affects relative prices, misallocations happen in the economy.

In order that prices fulfill their function as instruments of information and incentive, they must be flexible and responsive to changes in demand and supply. The concept of 'price stability' is a misplaced concept for this type of price changes. When the central bank speaks of 'price stability', the term does not refer to relative prices, but to the price level. The aim of the central bank is to keep the price index stable following the problematic concepts put forth by Irving Fisher and its current operation as inflation targeting.

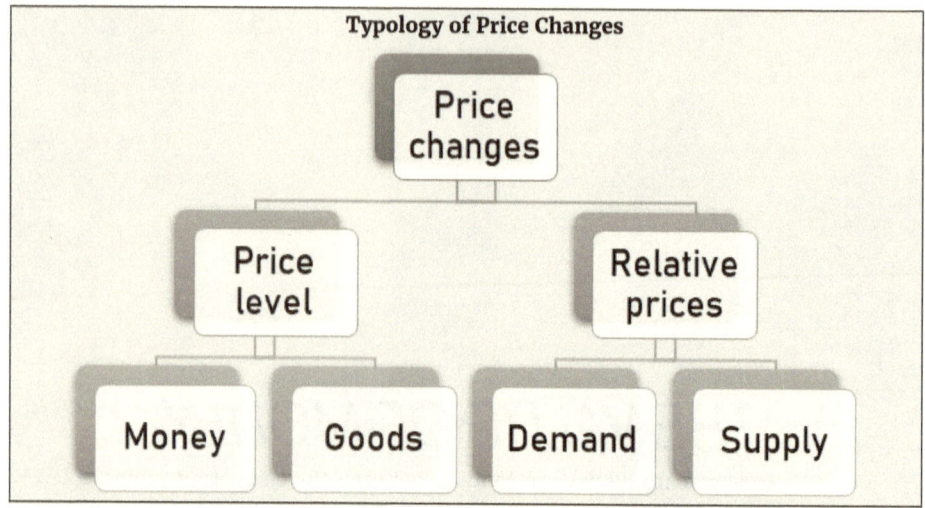

The published 'consumer price index' and the other price indices represent a statistical hodgepodge. One can concoct such statistics in many ways, and one can do this without violating common statistical rules. 'Hedonic calculation', which attempts to take account of changes in quality, is just one example.

But despite all the statistical tricks that are being invented and applied, the core issue remains unresolved: what is being measured by 'purchasing power' and what is the value of money—other than subjective and individualistic—upon which one could base the calculation?

Along with the statistics related to the figures about the domestic and national product, the price index is one of the most unreliable, most deceiving, and most abused statistical economic numbers. This is the case as the price index provides the basis for a series of other statistical indicators as it serves as a deflator and enters economic growth and productivity figures.

These macroeconomic numbers suffer from the illusion that one could observe the properties of an object—called 'the economy'—and could them measure. Whatever finesse will one applies to their calculation to make these statistics more accurate, it cannot do away with their basic invalidity that results from the impossibility of getting a fixed standard of measurement for value.

Attempts to measure the economy as if it were an object has its origin in government planning. Treating the economy as a whole becomes necessary for socialist central planners and for the economy of a country at war. Price indices and other statistics about macroeconomic variables are needed when some center with decision-making power wants to control the economy. Both 'fathers' of modern national income accounting, John Richard Nicholas Stone (Nobel Prize in economics 1984) and Simon Kuznets (Nobel Prize in economics in 1971) served in war planning offices where they developed and refined the concepts. Stone worked in the British government's War Cabinet Secretariat and Kuznets was Associate Director of the Bureau of Planning and Statistics and Director of Research at the Planning Committee of the U.S. War Production Board.

The results of these planning endeavors are well known; but while socialist-type total economic planning is off the screen even for many devout socialists, central monetary planning by manipulating money, credit, and the exchange rate ranks still high on the public agenda. Central banking is the last refuge for those under the spell of the pretense of knowledge.

Fixing their eyes on the so-called 'price stability' or following the now fashionable inflation targeting schemes, central bankers are not just after a movable target but one that is more symbolic than real. This way, they neglect the inflationary expansion of money and debt.

As with individual prices, the prices of groups of goods and services rise and fall. There are always inflationary and deflationary areas in an economy. When small aggregate price movements occur or when opposing forces are at work, the price index renders no valuable signal. If, however, strong tendencies in one or the other direction of the general price level are underway, and when this turns up in the price index, it is too late for the central banks to catch up.

Price indexes average out the extremes; they are unable to signal the subtler price movements and they leave out relevant items such as asset prices. This way, it is not only the public that is being deceived, the central banks themselves are falling victim to their calculations.

One need not resort to more extreme examples like how to measure today's musical output and compare it in a quality-adjusted form to that of the past. The measurement problem appears also when trying to give a percentage change in the output of software programs or administrative and engineering activities, not to speak of health, legal services, and education. The statisticians may answer that the 'measurement' of output is derived from expenditures. However, money prices measure nothing. Relative prices count as these inform the economic actor about the exchange ratios on the market.

As Ludwig von Mises (Human Action, 1998, p. 218) explained, '(t)he money equivalents as used in acting and in economic calculation are money prices, i.e., exchange ratios between money and other goods and services. The prices are not measured in money; they consist in money. Prices are either prices of the past or expected prices of the future. A price is necessarily a historical fact either of the past of the future. There is nothing in prices which permits one to liken them to the measurement of physical and chemical phenomena'.

Adding up all sales or compounding all assets in an economy eliminates the meaning of prices. This kind of aggregation differs from what a company or a person does when calculating profits or the relative wealth position. When a person adds up the prices of his various assets, he gets a number about his current wealth relative to the price universe he selects as his point of reference. For a company, it is sales, costs, and profits that matter, and for that sound business, one needs accounting. Neither for personal matters nor for business decisions GDP figures are necessary. Kuznets knew of the shortcomings of national income accounting, as his intention was to get a measure of overall well-being that would also include housework and leisure, a project that was doomed from the beginning in the eyes of the U.S. Department of Commerce when he assisted with the design of the national income statistics.

One can determine the weight of the overall output of some certain types of steel, but one cannot, in the same way, come to a reasonable result by measuring in one number the aggregate production of automobiles, of refrigerators, or of personal computers – not to speak about the problems one confronts when one tries to add up the output of teachers, nurses, songwriters or software programmers together with apples and oranges.

A company can count its production in terms of units of model M or T. If the company wants a figure for the total, it must resort to sales. Before sales, one can only enumerate how many units of each specific item category are in stock, and only by assuming that the company's products will catch certain prices, is it possible to calculate the expected monetary amount – but not the 'value' of production.

Mises explained it this way: 'Prices are always money prices, and costs cannot be taken into account in economic calculation if not expressed in terms of money. If one does not resort to terms of money, costs are expressed in complex quantities of diverse goods and services to be expended for the procurement of a product' (Mises, op. cit., p. 39). Likewise, one cannot add up values or valuations. 'One can add up prices expressed in terms of money, but not scales of preference.' (p. 332).

In a private market economy, the aims of economic activity are diverse and represent individual and subjective valuations. For an economy that is to serve multiple private needs, the measuring economic growth makes little sense, if any at all. One may add up nationwide the various monetary prices of the sold goods and services, but besides the aggregation of the monetary values of diverse items – what is the true and reliable informational value of this exercise?

Each good and service has a different value for each user. There is no common standard of value available. This is even more so the case when new products and new kinds of services come to the market. Valuations are not only heterogeneous among persons but also differ for the same person according to the specific circumstances. Human beings have different needs and desires in different situations, and they experience changes in taste. Preferences themselves are experimental devices.

Quality is not an attribute inherent to the things, but it is a valuation, which is imputed to the goods and services by the economic actor. Economic action aims to improve one's condition and what makes up an amelioration is subject to continuous change. Therefore, there is no objective way to measure overall wealth in aggregate form without coarse distortions and without violating the basic principles of economic valuation. Market prices 'are not expressive of equivalence, but of a divergence in the valuation of the two exchanging partners', and the value attached to the unit of supply is subject to the law of diminishing marginal utility (Mises, op. cit., p. 699).

It is the prerequisite of measurement that there must be identifiable objects in the measuring space and that a corresponding fixed standard of measuring unit can be applied. One can measure barrels of oil at the well and determine how much the production has grown or not. Measurement is per definition quantitative. In technical terms, one may measure quality by using technical standards such as that of crude oil, for example, based on its sulfur content, but this measurement is also quantitative. In this case, the measurement shows the usefulness of that good in terms of a criterion that comes from an industrial process. In the 1970s, it was the American economist Paul Samuelson (who was one of the first receivers of the fake Swedish Central Bank "Nobel Prize" in economic 'for his scientific work through which he has developed static and dynamic economic theory and contributed to raising the level of analysis in economic science') who never got tired to present a graph in the various editions of his popular economics textbook that showed that it would be just a matter of a few decades until the Soviet Union would take over the United States in 'production'. Of course, Soviet production figures were a humbug. Serious estimation, based on personal insight into the Soviet economy, come to a fraction of the official statistics (see Yuri Maltsev: https://fee.org/articles/soviet-economic-reforms-an-inside-perspective/).

Another phenomenon as reported by Richard Vedder (Statistical Malfeasance and Interpreting Economic Phenomena, in: The Review of Austrian Economics. Vol. 10, No. 2, 1997, pp. 77-89) refers to the calculated output decline for the U.S. economy in 1946. As later available statistics revealed, this contraction amounted to a fall of 20.6 percent of the gross domestic product. But this decline reflected the 'statistical fiction' that GDP was shrinking when in fact private employment and personal income were rising. The end of the wage-and-price controls meant a higher inflation rate, which in turn increased the recorded GDP price deflator (p. 82) and made the 'real production' statistically shrink. One may only wonder what the government would have done if the statistical information had already been available then.

END THE FED

Since its inception, modern central banking has gone through various fashions and has adopted opposing paradigms along the course of its history. The US Federal Reserve System began operating in January 1914 and stood ready to provide the monetary conditions for financing US entry into World War I.

Likewise, the US central bank provided the monetary ammunition for its government to fight in World War II and in the many other military conflicts that were to follow. In Europe, one of the first consequences of World War I was to abandon the gold standard and turning the central banks into the willing tools of governments.

In the early 1920s, the US central bank adopted Irving Fisher's proposal of using the consumer price index as the guide for monetary policy, ushering the economy first into an unsustainable economic boom and then into the Great Depression. In Europe, the Deutsche Reichsbank produced a hyperinflation in the early 1920s, and in the United Kingdom, the Bank of England toiled for decades without success against the economic slump. By the early 1930s, the political supremacy over central banking was complete. Irrespective of the degree of socialism, nationalism, and totalitarianism, the politicization of money and central banking encompassed the central banks from Moscow to Berlin, and from Paris to Washington and Tokyo. Central planning and interventionism had won the day.

After World War II, there was a short period when the so-called Bretton Woods System was firmly in place with the expectation that one held the philosopher's stone for monetary stability in one's hand. Establishing a link between the US dollar to gold and a fixed-exchange-rate system with an adjustable peg for its member countries to the dollar and thereby among themselves, the Bretton Woods System reflected the political power structure with the United States at the center, surrounded by the satellites.

Yet in the 1960s, Keynesianism became the dominant doctrine of central banking. Interest rates had to be low, so the mantra said, to stimulate investment and economic growth. Consequently, the United States government ignored its obligation to limit the dollar emission to the size of its gold stock, and the US central bank put no brakes on a further growth of the money supply. This policy led right into a decade of inflation first and stagflation later.

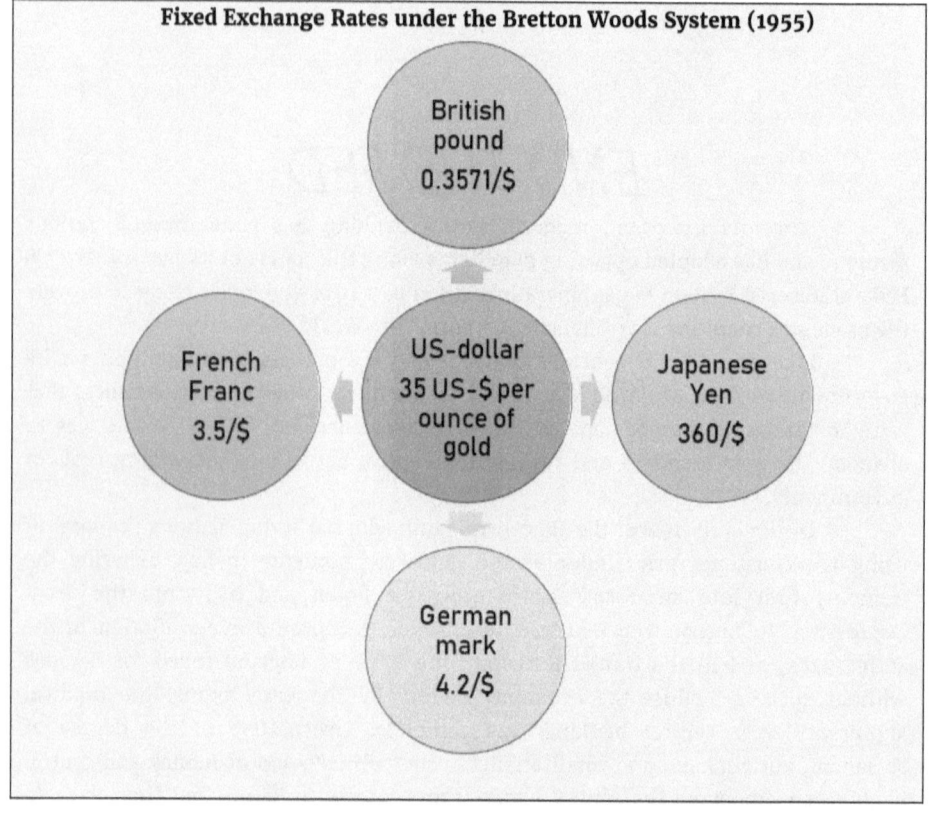

In West Germany, the 'Bank deutscher Länder' (later called 'Bundesbank') got its seat in Frankfurt and not in the capital city signaling a certain symbolic detachment from politics. The law that created the new German central bank obliged monetary policy to pursue 'price level stability'. Yet in the late 1960s and during the

1970s, inflation and then stagflation hit Germany and other European countries as well. One reason for that was the international monetary system itself, which obliged the member countries to stabilize their exchange rates against the US dollar.

The over-supply of dollars destroyed this system. The Bundesbank, along with other central banks in Europe and Japan, became the 'buyers of the last resort' for the weakening greenback. The world experienced a massive increase in liquidity originating from the US dollar that spilled over to the other major currencies. When the central banks in Europe and Japan bought dollars for their own currencies to stabilize the exchange rate, they expanded their domestic monetary base. After a short liquidity-driven boost, the world economy slipped into the stagflation of the 1970s.

The experience of stagflation led to a turnaround of monetary policy in the late 1970s when the US central bank embarked upon the monetarist experiment. Now, it was the money supply that became the magic word and the most important guideline for central banking. In the 1980s, price inflation rates declined. However, this happened more by accident than by design, because with the onset of the monetarist experiment, the velocity of money circulation — which had been trend-stable for decades — contracted.

Inadvertently, the restrictive monetary policy in place became contractive. In an ironic twist, the major tenet of monetarism — that the velocity of money would be stable or at least trend-stable — no longer held. This happened at that point when the central bankers adopted monetarism as their new credo. The recession of the early 1980s wiped out inflationary expectations. This result came not by design, but by a monetary policy error — an error, however, with beneficial results.

With Alan Greenspan (chairman of the Board of Governors of the Federal Reserve System from 1987 to 2006), the US central bank abandoned monetarism and went on to the next fashion: supply-side economics. Greenspan liked to look at productivity growth as the guideline and the money-supply number became less important. His doctrine said that a central bank can expand the monetary base and have low policy rates when productivity in the economy is rising. This laid the groundwork for the great financial-asset boom of the 1990s. The chairman became the darling of Wall Street, its guru, and the oracle to listen to, and the reliable bail-out guarantor as the man of the last resort for the financial markets.

In Asia, meanwhile, the Japanese central bank produced first an unsustainable economic boom in the 1980s, then instigated the crash of 1989–90, and has tried to re-inflate the economy ever since. In the 1980s, the Japanese central bank saw no need to curb the booming stock and real-estate markets because the price index remained stable, and Japan was seemingly on its way to becoming 'Number One'. The Bank of Japan boosted its monetary base in the 1980s, and after the bust, it lowered its policy rate almost to zero. While the expected recovery did not happen, the Bank of Japan provided a bonanza for financial speculators who practice the yen-carry-trade by borrowing at low-interest rates in Japan and lending at higher interest rates abroad.

Europe introduced a common currency in 1999. The statutes of the European Central Bank (ECB) called for a clear priority of 'price stability' as the guideline for monetary policy. The seat of the European Central Bank is in Frankfurt, Germany, almost equidistant to Brussels, which hosts the executive branch of the European Union, and to Strasbourg, where the European Parliament resides, thus symbolizing that the ECB should be independent and free of political influence.

The autonomy of the ECB has a quasi-constitutional status within the European legal framework. Thus, it remained to be seen what would happen when more serious challenges arise in the euro system. And indeed: instead of risking the departure of a member state in financial trouble, the ECB acted like any other central bank and boosted the money supply according to the central bankers' motto: *après nous le deluge* in the face of the European debt crisis, which began in 2010.

In the United States, Ben Bernanke has been the chairman of the Board of Governors of the US Federal Reserve System from 2006 to 2014. He, too, is an adherent of inflation targeting, yet the US central bank is not explicit about what definite desired rate of inflation (as it is measured by the consumer price index) should be its goal.

The concept of inflation targeting is not new. It has its origins in Irving Fisher's monetary theory. By following this monetary policy concept, the US central bank created the boom of the late 1920s and the great bust. Nevertheless, this theory is now experiencing a revival in Europe and the United States.

The monetary policy concept of inflation targeting suffers from the fundamental problem that a valid price index does not exist. There is no such a thing as a representative basket of goods and services. Fisher's idea was already problematic in the simpler economy of the 1920s; nowadays it is outright obsolete to establish an index that could represent the complex and diverse economy as it exists today. Each individual person has his specific basket of goods and services, and its composition will change for the same individual.

Although a valid price index does not exist, central bankers use this indicator as a guideline to plan a monetary policy that affects the whole economy. Irving Fisher is back, center stage, in the person of Ben Bernanke and his successor Janet Yellen (chairwomen from 2014 to 2018). These two sell their inflation-targeting concept as something new, when in fact it is the rehash of Irving Fisher's theory — a theory that both the facts of history and the economic theory of the Austrian School have discredited.

THE DEBACLE OF ECONOMIC STABILIZATION POLICIES

The record of modern central banking is bleak. Serving as a bailout machine for the financial markets and as a reliable financier of the state, modern central banks by the nature of their origin and existence do not curb the booms (which they could) and do not prevent recessions or depressions (which they would wish to do but cannot). Monetary policy suffers from the same faults as any other centralized economic policy and other forms of interventionism, and like all centralized economic policies and interventionist measures, the monetary policy of active central banks has been failing again and again.

Modern economies are too complex and diverse for central control. The more complex and diverse the economy gets, the more the data will have to be compressed, finally to such a degree that they lose their meaning and become useless at best and misleading at worst as informational tools for decision-making. For monetary policy, which acts like a central-planning agency when it comes to the money supply and the interest rate, the informational quality of the data that central banks use is deteriorating. Aggregates and averages such as the Gross Domestic Product or the inflation rate, productivity growth, or the many other economic indicators that are so popular nowadays with central bankers and the financial press and in econometric studies, hide more than they reveal and are often misleading for decision-making and economic analysis.

Given that there are no constant quantitative relations among the variables, central bankers have no reliable guideline to calibrate their monetary policy measures. One cannot know for sure how monetary impulses transform economic activity and to which degree the monetary streams affect consumer prices or how they will change investment or impact upon asset prices. How the monetary transmission mechanism has worked, shows up in retrospect, and the results are valid only for a specific period.

Research of statistical relations is history. The results provide no certainty about how the transmission mechanism will work in the future. The monetary impulse coming from the monetary base can transform into various degrees of strengths depending on the money multiplier and the velocity of circulation, and from there it can change the components of the real economy. It all depends on the individual human action; and human expectations, plans, and actions change over time, sometimes drastically.

Statistical aggregates per se cause nothing in the economy. What is being measured by the aggregates and averages are the effects of human action, and not their causes. There is no way to know ex-ante whether a specific monetary policy measure affects the so-called price level of final goods — whether the main effect goes into the asset market, or leads to more investment at home, or more imports from abroad. Central bankers do not know whether changes in the money supply and the interest rate will cause a change of credit demand for business investment or a change of credit demand for private and public consumption.

Central bankers sometimes describe their activity as 'more art than science', which is the implicit recognition of their ignorance. The 'art of central banking' is the virtuosity of pretending to know what one does not know. Not only is it not a science; it is not even an art. It is alchemy at best and a gigantic cheat at worst.

When economic systems grow in complexity and diversity, central planning and interventionism become inefficient, and the need arises for more decentralized coordination mechanisms. Modern economies and modern financial markets have become too complex for an active central banking. It is an illusion to believe that more research and better central bankers could improve monetary policy. One needs something else: a monetary system that works without an active central bank.

The world needs a new monetary system. The reform must consist in the de-nationalization of central banking and establishing a private banking system. To deprive the central banks of its power, it suffices to freeze the basic money - the part of the money, which a central bank controls - and to allow a free banking system.

According to this plan, the supply of central bank money – the so-called monetary base – would be fixed at a specific amount. This will limit the range of inflation and contraction of macroeconomic liquidity and thus eliminate a central factor of the major cyclical fluctuations. A complete economic stability, as the politicians once promised, has never been attainable anyway, and it is not even desirable. Even if the volume of the monetary base no longer varies, fluctuations (because of changes in velocity of circulation) would still occur, as it is necessary for a dynamic economy. What is important, however, is to limit the extreme economic swings of boom and bust. The freezing of the money supply (the central bank's monetary base) would be a crucial step to curtail the possibilities of money-induced economic cycles. When there is a fixed amount of central bank money, the commercial banks will be cautious in lending and will restrain unsound booms. A constant amount of the monetary base combined with a free banking system ties the monetary system to a fixed anchor and makes the economy more stable without impeding the monetary flexibility. Under such a monetary system, macroeconomic liquidity - and thus nominal national income - would still vary within limits because of the elasticity of the monetary multiplier and the velocity of the circulation of money.

THE CRISIS OF 2008

The financial crisis of 2008 did not come from anywhere. Its basis was laid over a long period with the welfare state, the inflation of money and the adoption of the Keynesian economic policy framework as the new orthodoxy. The great American boom since the 1980s was built on monetary expansion, low-interest rates, and a relentless policy of bailouts when the bubbles burst. The result has been the build-up of unsustainable debt burdens. When debt accumulation hit its limit in the private sector and in the banking system, and when markets began 'to freeze', governments jumped in with bailout guarantees and stimulus packages, which only added a fiscal crisis on top of the financial market and economic crisis.

Excessive monetary expansion and the resulting low-interest rates represent the immediate causes of the crisis of 2008. At a deeper level, however, lies the current monetary system. The structure that emerged after the breakdown of the Bretton Woods system in 1971 is cut off from what was left of an anchor. The new monetary schemes have become an engine of debt expansion of the private and the public sector. It is a system devoid of a mechanism that would curb debt expansion in time. The current monetary arrangements allow central banks to make the debt accumulation go on until the final collapse.

The crisis of 2008 and thereafter is as much a financial as an economic crisis and most of all it is a crisis of indebtedness. This excess of debt includes households and governments, and it includes the external balances, the persistent current account deficits of the United States, which, as their counterpart, imply the accumulation of surpluses in China, some other Asian, and of European countries.

What began as a banking crisis and diagnosed as the result of 'too little regulation' has its origin in the notion of central bankers that the problem is 'too little inflation'. The inflationary acts of central banks and governments are at the origin of the troubles that spill over from the financial sector to the real economy. What began as excessive money supply and has produced excessive debt, is now showing up in slow growth and stagnant incomes.

With economic policies, there is often a considerable time lag between the phase when one plants the seeds and the phase when the harvest will come - between cause and effect. In the case of the financial and economic crisis of 2008, the time of planting goes back to the 1960s and 1970s, when the welfare state became the new creed in the Western world, when economic policy adopted Keynesianism, and when the last remnants of the gold standard were removed.

The late 1960s experienced the start of the drastic expansion of the welfare state, and in the early 1970s, the rest of what had remained of a sound monetary system was abandoned. Adopting the Keynesian economic policy model would make the triad complete.

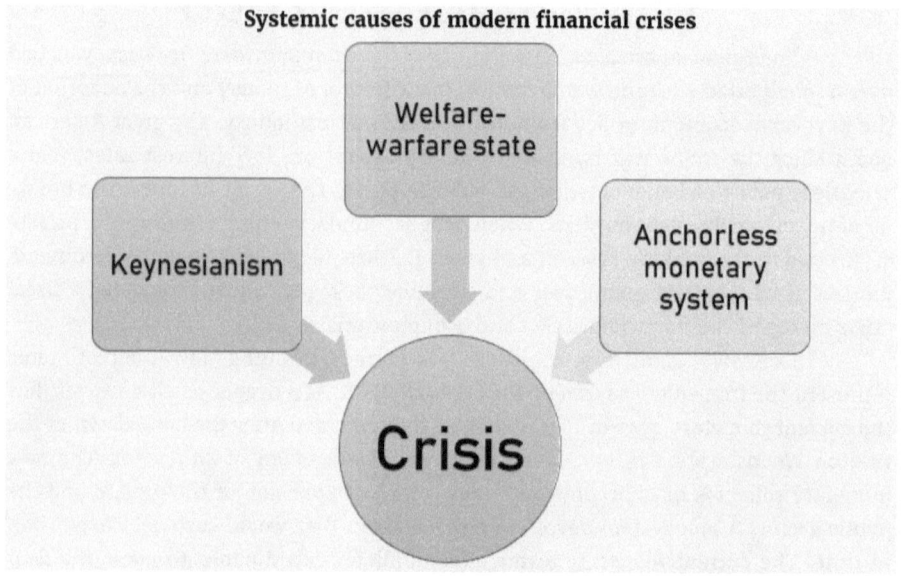

The new consensus encompasses an unhampered expansion of the welfare state, an activist discretionary monetary policy without anchor or definite rules and the economic policy of vulgar Keynesianism with its false promise that government had the tools to lift a country to prosperity and full employment through government spending and easy money.

It did not take long until this kind of policy produced its first disaster: stagflation. Facing the result of the Keynesian politics in the rise of unemployment, economic stagnation, and inflation demand for a new economic policy paradigm arose, and it was found in "monetarism". Monetarism, however, as an economic policy concept, was in some respects an even more simplified version of Keynesianism. Despite its promotion of free markets, there was little true classical economics in the monetarist model. When monetarists declared 'we're all Keynesians now', it meant much more than an ironic twist.

When Reaganomics – the economic policy of President Reagan and his promotion to combine tax cuts and deregulation – came along in the early 1980s, this economic policy failed with its promise to reduce government expenditure. While the American central bank under Paul Volcker brought down the inflation rate and while unemployment fell, government deficits swelled, and the public debt increased to new highs. That was the time when the slogan emerged 'deficits don't matter'.

In this respect, the new economic ideology of 'supply side economics' had become even more Keynesian. Now, the original idea of anti-cyclical public finance was put aside. The governments abandoned the principle that cuts of public expenditure and budget surpluses would be required in good economic times to have the funds to spend when the economy would turn into a recession. The new economic policy consensus says deficits would not matter, and thus that one can ignore the debt levels and neglect the exchange rate of the dollar because central banks were capable of managing the monetary side of the economy.

What was called 'The Great Moderation', and as it was believed by central bankers to be the case, is a macroeconomic constellation, which does not guarantee that the economy is sound. Besides the uncertainties of measuring economic growth and the price index, limiting the theoretical focus only on these two indicators deceives.

The Keynesian-monetarist synthesis that dominated economic policy actions during the decades from the 1980s onwards, stopped paying attention to credit growth and debt accumulation. In the run-up to the crisis of 2008, monetary policy ignored that household liabilities had risen by a factor of 14 since the early 1980s and reached 14 trillion at the outbreak of the current crisis (Data-FRED. https://fred.stlouisfed.org/series/CMDEBT#0)

As long as price inflation seemed under control, the monetary policy concept of the New Keynesians no longer asked what kind of economic growth was happening if macroeconomic statistics registered the expansion of real gross domestic product. What was called 'Great Moderation' and what was experienced as a decades-long boom should better be called a gigantic bubble whose creation and maintenance resulted from the dedicated application of bailout economics by the major central banks of the world.

While a bailout may be beneficial in the individual case and is so for the persons who receive the bailout money, bailouts have systemic consequences: Over time, each new bailout will add to the level of moral hazard and after a series of bailouts, moral hazard will become systemic. What at first is a benign government gift, over time will become a manifest expectation, and bailouts will be nothing less than the rightful claims on government money.

Bailouts produce a moral hazard and this way risk perception will approach diminish. Without the restraint of financial losses, an overexpansion of commercial activities will occur. Bailouts institutionalize perverse risk behavior, and it is not before long that the new aggressive attitude will rule across the board by the business community and by the financial market operators. In fact, bailouts impose a negative selection mechanism where prudence gets punished. With risk perception taken out of business life, the economic expansion means that a growing part of the resulting economic growth exists in unsustainable investments. This, in turn, implies that most of the economic activity that comes as the result of falling risk perception amounts to the squandering of capital. In relation to the point of departure, the economy that appears to be on the path of prosperity is getting poorer. When the bubble pops, the level of prosperity is lower than it was before the false boom. After a decade since the bubble burst, there has not yet been a full recovery, while the new bubble is ready to pop.

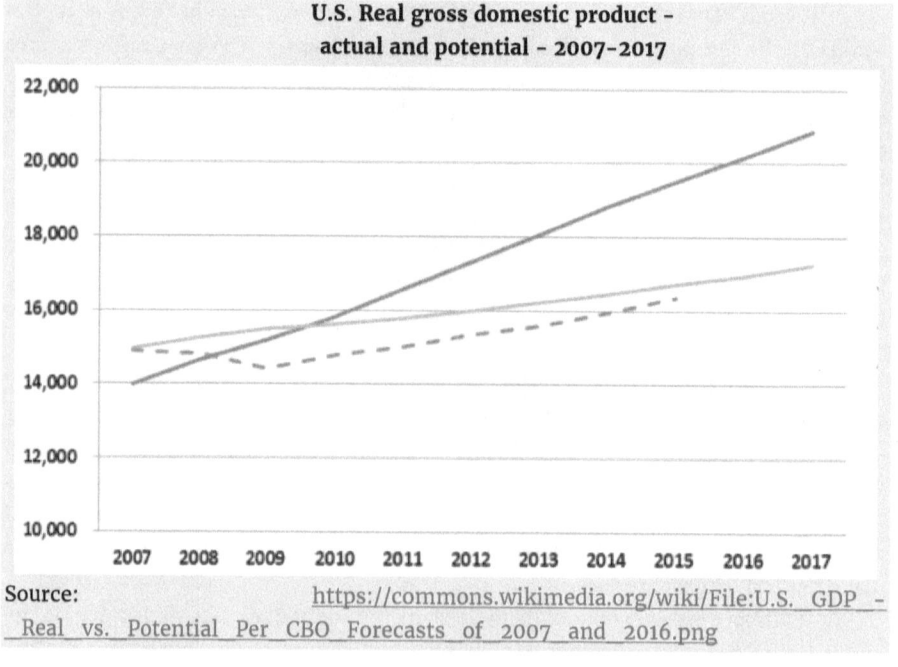

Source: https://commons.wikimedia.org/wiki/File:U.S._GDP_-_Real_vs._Potential_Per_CBO_Forecasts_of_2007_and_2016.png

The graph shows in descending order

- the projection of potential gross domestic product (gdp) of the Congressional Budget Office (CBO) in 2017 (red line)
- the estimation and projection of potential gdp of the CBO in 2016 (green line)
- the performance of action gdp (dotted blue line)

***

The so-called 'New Economy' of the 1990s led to stock market prices that exceeded all conventional measures in terms of price-earnings-ratios. Public initial offerings by companies that lacked earnings and sometimes even a product (the only thing they had was a business plan) achieved extreme valuations at the stock market and produced short-term billionaires overnight. Of course, there was hype; there was gullibility, and there was greed involved. Yet these emotions do not fall from the blue sky. In fact, 'irrational exuberance' had a broad basis: liquidity. The same persons who lamented irrationality were the relentless pushers of liquidity.

Flooding the markets with more money provided the basis for the kick-in of the wealth effect due to the rising participation of the population in the stock market through investment funds and 401k accounts. The result was a period of illusionary prosperity. Low-interest rates and ample tax revenues coming from capital appreciation let it even appear for some time as if government debt would disappear.

The financial crisis of 2008 has its origin in excessive lending, which, in turn, is due to a monetary system whose basis is debt.

Due to insufficient domestic savings, the United States has accumulated a net foreign investment position that has reached over eight trillion US dollars. The United States has turned from the world's largest creditor at the end of World War II into the world's largest debtor nation. In addition to its precarious foreign investment position, the US government, when confronted with the outbreak of the financial crisis, has intervened in the private market and taken up positions with financial institutions and major companies close to bankruptcy. At the same time, the US central bank has acted as a lender of the last resort. Along with lowering the Federal Funds Rate, the US central bank has bought up junk papers from the private banking sector and extended its balance sheet with poisonous assets.

The financial situation of the US consumer has become unsustainable. It is illusionary to expect a recovery beginning with consumption. Fiscal expansion and loose monetary policies have achieved extreme proportions. Interest rate policy has touched 'zero bound', and government debt and the foreign debt position of the United States have reached critical levels.

Like in Japan over the past decades, with its ongoing fiscal expansion and loose monetary policy, the positive effect on economic growth of the stimulus packages in the United States has been meager and is petering out.

The current international monetary structure is more a 'non-system' than a system or an order. It does not provide a sound monetary order. Interventionist systems, like the one that is now in existence for monetary matters, drive towards their own dissolution. It seems as if the end stage of the interventionist spiral has come full circle considering that the starting point of the modern interventionist state existed in getting hold of money creation. It is the sovereign authority over money that provides the conditions of the welfare-warfare state and the rise of the modern interventionist state.

The economic and financial crisis of 2008 and its aftermath have exposed the modern monetary system as a mechanism of debt expansion whose inherent dynamics move this system to the limit. The structure of the modern monetary system in its combination with modern populist democracy produces the dynamics which drives it to hyperinflation or bankruptcy. Deflation is the main concern of the monetary authorities' because a falling price level means bankruptcy. Because of the irrational 'fear of deflation', the central bankers work as hard as they can to create debt inflation in order to lift the price level. Yet in as much as they succeed in promoting debt inflation, the final stage will be bankruptcy. Instead of letting the system go the shortcut to deflation and from there to bankruptcy, monetary authorities promote a detour from debt inflation to bankruptcy, and from bankruptcy to deflation. Most of all, however, the modern interventionist policy measures aimed at avoiding any recession and thus prone to prevent a re-positioning of the economy to correct the past errors, produce widening distortions of the capital structures. What one or two decades ago could have been resolved by a short recession does require a much costlier process of adaptation.

Economic policy intervention in the form of bailouts creates a systemic moral hazard that for some time helped to avoid an economic downturn. Yet after that, there will be a collapse much harsher than anything that would have happened earlier it the policymakers had left the economy by itself to adapt.

2008 marks not a crisis of capitalism but a crisis of state interventionism. To get rid of future episodes of this kind, more regulations will not help. On the contrary. Crisis prevention requires the end of the policy of bailouts. If not, the monetary system gets even more perverted. Yet more regulations become necessary – not because markets do not work, but because there are already too many interventions and too many regulations in place. More regulation does not prevent the crises but lays the groundwork for them to happen.

THE DEBACLE OF ECONOMIC STABILIZATION POLICIES

SUMMARY

Fluctuations are part of the economy. Instability by itself is not harmful. Likewise, stability is not always beneficial. Dynamic systems, like a market economy, work on the principle of error and correction. The faster one can correct allocative errors, the better for the system. The individual parts of the economic order must have the freedom to adapt. For the economy, this principle bears the name 'Laissez-faire. It is therefore important to allow the self-healing powers of the market economy to come to the fore.

At no stage of the cycle do the economic policymakers know which course the economy will take. It is thus impossible to calibrate the measures or even to determine in advance whether the economy needs a stimulant or a sedative. There is no way to know in which direction the economy will move. The forecasting techniques are useless, especially to determine turning points. If everything remains as it is, one does not need a forecast; if one needed a prediction because things change, the prognosis techniques do not work. Policymakers grope in the dark even if they do not admit it.

Instead of economic policy, one needs to apply measures that make the economy more flexible and adaptable. This includes, first, dismantling regulations and reducing the tax burden. Besides the uncertainty already created in the economic process itself, activist economic policy adds another element of uncertainty. The individual economic decision-makers must pay attention to what is changing in the economy and, additionally, what policymakers will do.

Political uncertainty can mean that the economy freezes on a large scale. Economic policymakers then speak of a weak economy. The regret the loss of the spirit of enterprise. These economic policymakers themselves, however, caused the uncertainty and thus the economic paralysis. The rise of uncertainty because of politics was one of the main causes of the Great Depression. Now, a new wave of political hyper-activism is taking place.

Antony P. Mueller

FIGURES AND TABLES

- Economic growth of the United States since 1789
- Consumer prices and unemployment
- Stagflation characteristics
- Deflationary and inflationary gaps
- Problems of Keynesianism
- Say's Law of Supply and demand
- Determinants of employment
- Price-wage spiral
- Monetarist, Keynesian, and Neo-Classical types of economic contractions
- Keynesian sequence
- Neo-Classical sequence
- Monetarism's unresolved issues
- Velocity of circulation, 1928-2016
- Japan. Policy interest rate and public debt ratio
- Labor productivity since 1950 of selected countries
- Idealized Keynesian public debt cycle
- Ratchet effect of public debt
- Main forms of anti-capitalism
- Types of business cycle models
- Marxist crisis model
- Keynesian crisis model
- Post-Keynesian crisis model
- Model of the New Keynesians
- Schumpeter's model of the business cycle
- Real business cycle model
- Neoclassical model
- Monetarist model
- Model of the Austrian business cycle theory
- Model of the capital-based credit cycle
- Stylized general business cycle
- Cascade of policy failures
- Policy measures of the New Deal
- International financial obligations after World War I
- Dawes and Young Plans
- Kindleberger spiral of international trade
- Economic indicators of the Great Depression
- United States. Great Depression Data 1929-1940

- US Real Gross Domestic Product, 1929-1940
- US Civilian Unemployment Rate, 1929,1940
- US Consumer Price Index, 1929-1940
- German economy. Growth and inflation 1926-1939
- Rothbard's Do's and Don'ts in a depression
- Misery index
- Inflation and deflation mechanism
- Deflation. Types and causes
- Inflation - Types and causes
- Deflation and inflation in the United States since 1775
- Purchasing power of the US dollar, 1913-2017
- German hyperinflation, monetary base and wholesale price index
- US consumer price index, 1950-2017
- Global money creation by the major central banks
- US personal debt structure
- Average Annual Rates of Labor and Capital Productivity Growth, 1899-1937
- US consumer price index, 1914-1930
- US bank lending, 1920-1939
- US Federal reserve monetary base, 1986-2017
- Main objectives of macroeconomic policy
- Instruments of macroeconomic policy
- Typology of price changes
- Systemic causes of modern financial crises
- Liabilities of households and non-profit organizations, 1980-2008
- United Stages money supply, 1980-2008
- U.S. Real gross domestic product - actual and potential, 2007-2017

BIBLIOGRAPHICAL REFERENCES

Achen, Christopher H. and Larry M. Bartels: Democracy for Realists: Why Elections Do Not Produce Responsive Government (Princeton Studies in Political Behavior) Princeton University Press 2017

Antonopoulos, Andreas M.: The Internet of Money. Merkle Bloom LLC. 2016

Applebaum, Anne: Gulag. A History. Anchor Books. 2004

Applebaum, Anne: Red Famine: Stalin's War on the Ukraine. Doubleday. 2017

Ashford, Nigel and Stephen Davis (eds.): A Dictionary of Conservative and Libertarian Thought (Routledge Revivals). Routledge. 2012

Bagus, Philipp: In Defense of Deflation (Financial and Monetary Policy Studies). Springer 2014

Bagus, Phillipp and Andreas Marquart: Blind Robbery!: How the Fed, Banks and Government Steal Our Money. FinanzBuch Verlag. 2016

Baldwin, Richard: The Great Convergence: Information Technology and the New Globalization. Belknap Press. 2016

Banerjee, Abhijit, and Esther Duflo: Poor Economics: A Radical Rethinking of the Way to Fight Global Poverty. Public Affairs. 2012

Barnett, Anthony: The Athenian Option: Radical Reform for the House of Lords (Sortition and Public Policy Book 5). Imprint Academic. 2017

Barrat, James: Our Final Invention: Artificial Intelligence and the End of the Human Era. St Martin's Griffin. 2015

Belke, Ansgar and Thorsten Polleit: Monetary Economics in Globalised Financial Markets. Springer. 2009

Belloc, Hilaire: The Servile State. T. N. Foulis 1912

Benda, Julien: The Treason of the Intellectuals. Routledge. 2006

Benson, Bruce L: The Enterprise of Law: Justice Without the State. Independent Institute. 2011

Birner, Jack and Pierre Garrouste (eds): Markets, Information and Communication: Austrian Perspectives on the Internet Economy (Routledge Foundations of the Market Economy). Routledge. 2003

Block, Walter: Defending the Undefendable. Ludwig von Mises Institute. 2008

Block, Walter: The Privatization of Roads and Highways: Human and Economic Factors. CreateSpace Independent Publishing Platform. 2012

Block, Walter: Toward a Libertarian Society. Ludwig von Mises Institute. 2014

Boaz, David (ed.). The Libertarian Reader: Classic & Contemporary Writings from Lao-Tzu to Milton Friedman. Simon & Schuster 2015

Boaz, David: The Libertarian Mind. A Manifesto for Freedom. Simon & Schuster. 2015

Boehm-Bawerk, Eugen von: Karl Marx and the Close of His System: A Criticism (Classic Reprint). Forgotten Books. 2012

Boehm-Bawerk, Eugen von: Positive Theory of Capital. Ludwig von Mises Institute. 2007

Bostroum, Nick: Superintelligence: Paths, Dangers, Strategies. Oxford University Press 2016

Boetie, Etienne de la: The Politics of Obedience: The Discourse of Voluntary Servitude. With an Introduction by Murray Rothbard. Ludwig von Mises Insitute. 2015

Boettke, Peter J.: Living Economics: Yesterday, Today, and Tomorrow (Independent Studies in Political Economy). Independent Institute. 2012

Boettke, Peter J.: Calculation and Coordination: Essays on Socialism and Transitional Political Economy (Routledge Foundations of the Market Economy). Routledge 2001

Boettke, Peter J.: The Oxford Handbook of Austrian Economics (Oxford Handbooks). Oxford University Press. 2015

Boettke, Peter J.: The Political Economy of Soviet Socialism: the Formative Years, 1918-1928. 1990th Edition. Springer 1990

Boldrin, Michele and David K. Levine. Against Intellectual Monopoly. Cambridge University Press. 2010

Bourdieu, Pierre: On the State: Lectures at the College de France, 1989 - 1992. Polity 2015

Bouricius, Terry: (S)election: Sortition, the democratic alternative (Fomite Interrogations: A Series of Tracts for Our Time) (Volume 6). Fomite Publishers 2017

Boyes, William J.: Managerial Economics: Markets and the Firm (Upper Level Economics Titles). South-Western College Publications. 2011

Brafman, Ori and Rod A. Becksstrom: The Starfish and the Spider: The Unstoppable Power of Leaderless Organizations. Portfolio. 2008

Brafman, Ori and Rod A. Becksstrom: The Starfish and the Spider: The Unstoppable Power of Leaderless Organizations. Portfolio. 2008

Brackins, Daniel Alexander: Private Property, the Law, and the State. CreateSpace Independent Publishing Platform. 2017

Braun, Eduard: Finance behind the Veil of Money. CreateSpace Independent Publishing Platform. 2016

Brennan, Jason: Against Democracy. Princeton University Press. 2016

Brick, Howard: *Transcending Capitalism: Visions of a New Society in Modern American Thought.* Cornell University Press. 2016

Brynjolfsson, Eric and Andrew McAfee: *The Second Machine Age: Work, Progress, and Prosperity in a Time of Brilliant Technologies.* W. W. Norton & Company. 2016

Buchanan, James and Richard Wagner: *Democracy in Deficit. The Legacy of Lord Keynes.* Emerald Group Publishing. 1977

Burnheim, John: *The Demarchy Manifesto. For Better Public Policy* (Societas). Imprint Academic 2016

Burnheim, John: *Is Democracy Possible? The Alternative to Electoral Politics.* University of California Press. 1985

Burnheim, John: *The Demarchy Manifesto: For Better Public Policy* (Societas). Imprint Academic. 2016

Bylund, Per L.: *The Problem of Production: A new theory of the firm.* Routledge 2015

Cachanosky, Nicolas: *Monetary Equilibrium and Nominal Income Targeting* (Routledge International Studies in Money and Banking). Routledge. 2018

Caplan, Bryan: *The Case against Education: Why the Education System Is a Waste of Time and Money.* Princeton University Press. 2018

Caplan, Bryan: *The Myth of the Rational Voter: Why Democracies Choose Bad Policies.* Princeton University Press. 2008

Chafuen, Alejandro A.: *Faith and Liberty: The Economic Thought of the Late Scholastics* (Studies in Ethics and Economics). Lexington Books. 2003

Christinsen, Clayton M.: *The Innovator's Dilemma: When New Technologies Cause Great Firms to Fail* (Management of Innovation and Change). Harvard Business Review Press. 2016

Clark, Gregory: *A Farewell to Alms: A Brief Economic History of the World* (The Princeton Economic History of the Western World). Princeton University Press. 2009

Cogan, John F.: *The High Cost of Good Intentions: A History of U.S. Federal Entitlement Programs.* Princeton University Press. 2017

Conquest, Robert: *The Great Terror: A Reassessment* 40th anniversary Edition. Oxford University Press. 2007

Conquest, Robert: *The Harvest of Sorrow: Soviet Collectivization and the Terror-Famine.* Oxford University Press; Reprint edition. 1987

Cowen, Tyler and Alex Tabarrok: *Modern Principles of Economics.* Worth Publishers. 2014

Cowen, Tyler: *Average Is Over: Powering America Beyond the Age of the Great Stagnation.* Plume. 2014

Cowen, Tyler: The Great Stagnation: *How America Ate All the Low-Hanging Fruit of Modern History, Got Sick, and Will (Eventually) Feel Better.* Dutton 2011

Coyne, Christopher J. and Abigail R. Hall: *Tyranny Comes Home: The Domestic Fate of U.S. Militarism.* Stanford University Press. 2018

Cwick, Paul F.: *An Investigation of Inverted Yield Curves and Economic Downturns.* Ludwig von Mises Institute.

Dahlen, Michael: Ending Big Government: The Essential Case for Capitalism and Freedom. Mill City Press. 2016

Dalrymple, Theodore: Nothing but Wickedness: The Origins of the Decline of Our Culture. Gibson Square Books. 2018

Davidson, James Dale and William Rees-Mogg: The Sovereign Individual: Mastering the Transition to the Information Age. Touchstone. 1999

Delannoi, Gil and Oliver Dowlen (eds.): Sortition: Theory and Practice (Sortition and Public Policy). Imprint Academic. 2010

Deneen, Patrick J.: Why Liberalism Failed (Politics and Culture). Yale University Press. 2018

Diamandis, Peter H. and Steven Kotler: Abundance: The Future Is Better Than You Think. Free Press. Reprint edition. 2014

Di Iorio, Francesco: Cognitive Autonomy and Methodological Individualism: The Interpretative Foundations of Social Life (Studies in Applied Philosophy, Epistemology and Rational Ethics). Springer 2015

Dilorenzo Thomas J.: How Capitalism Saved America: The Untold History of Our Country, from the Pilgrims to the Present. Crown Forum. 2005

Dilorenzo, Thomas: The Problem with Socialism. Regnery Publishing. 2016

Doherty, Brian: Radicals for Capitalism: A Freewheeling History of the Modern American Libertarian Movement. Public Affairs. 2008

Dorn, James A. (ed.): Monetary Alternatives: Rethinking Government Fiat Money. Cato Institute 2017

Dorn, James A., Steve H. Hanke and Alan A. Sir Walters (eds.); The Revolution in Development Economics. Cato Institute. 1998

Dowlen, Oliver: The Political Potential of Sortition: A study of the random selection of citizens for public office (Sortition and Public Policy). Imprint Academic 2009

Drochon, Hugo: Nietzsche's Great Politics. Princeton University Press. 2016

Drucker, Peter: Innovation and Entrepreneurship. HarperBusiness. 2006

Easterbrook, Gregg: It's Better Than It Looks: Reasons for Optimism in an Age of Fear. PublicAffairs. 2018

Easterly, William R.: The Elusive Quest for Growth: Economists' Adventures and Misadventures in the Tropics. The MIT Press. 2002

Easterly, William: The White Man's Burden: Why the West's Efforts to Aid the Rest Have Done So Much Ill and So Little Good. Penguin. 2007

Easterly, William R.: The Tyranny of Experts: Economists, Dictators, and the Forgotten Rights of the Poor. Basic Books. 2015

Ebeling, Richard and Jacob G. Hornberger: The Failure of America's Foreign Wars. Future of Freedom Foundation. 1996

Ebeling, Richard M.: Monetary Central Planning and the State. The Future of Freedom Foundation. 2015

Emerson, Ralph Waldo: The Essential Writings of Ralph Waldo Emerson (Modern Library Classics). Modern Library. 2000

Eire, N. N. Carlos: Reformations: The Early Modern World, 1450-1650. Yale University Press. 2016

Eucken, Walter: The Foundations of Economics: History and Theory in the Analysis of Economic Reality. Springer. 2011

Eusepi, Guiseppe and Richard E. Wagner: Public Debt: An Illusion of Democratic Political Economy (New Thinking in Political Economy series). Edward Elgar Publications. 2017

Erhard, Ludwig: Prosperity Through Competition. Praeger. 1958

Ertel, Wolfgang: Introduction to Artificial Intelligence (Undergraduate Topics in Computer Science). Springer 2018

Evans, Anthony J.: Markets for Managers: A Managerial Economics Primer (The Wiley Finance Series). Wiley. 2014

Evans, Michelle and Augusto Zimmermann(eds.): Global Perspectives on Subsidiarity (Ius Gentium: Comparative Perspectives on Law and Justice). Springer 2014

Evans, Stanton M.: Stalin's Secret Agents: The Subversion of Roosevelt's Government. Threshold Editions. 2013

Ebeling, Richard: Austrian Economics and Public Policy. Restoring Freedom and Prosperity. The Future of Freedom Foundation. 2016

Ferguson, Niall: The Square and the Tower: Networks and Power, from the Freemasons to Facebook. Penguin Press. 2018

Ferguson, Niall: Civilization: The West and the Rest. Penguin Books. 2012

Fareed, Zakaria: The Future of Freedom: Illiberal Democracy at Home and Abroad (Revised Edition). W. W. Norton & Company. 2007

Feyerabend, Paul: Against Method. Verso. 2010

Folsom, Burton W.: The Myth of the Robber Barons: A New Look at the Rise of Big Business in America. Young America Foundation. 1991

Ford, Martin: The Rise of the Robots: Technology and the Threat of a Jobless Future. Basic Book. Reprint edition. 2015

Foss, Nikolai J. and Peter Klein (eds.): Entrepreneurship and the Firm: Austrian Perspectives on Economic Organization. Edward Elgar Publishing. 2002

Frank, Malcolm, Paul Roehrig, Ben Pring: What To Do When Machines Do Everything: How to Get Ahead in a World of AI, Algorithms, Bots, and Big Data. Wiley 2017

Friedman, David D.: The Machinery of Freedom: Guide to Radical Capitalism. CreateSpace Independent Publishing Platform; 3rd edition. 2015

Friedman, Milton and Anna Jacobson Schwartz: A Monetary History of the United States, 1867-1960. Princeton University Press. 1971

Friedman, Milton: Capitalism and Freedom. Fortieth Anniversary Edition. University of Chicago Press. 2002

Fukuyama, Francis: The Origins of Political Order: From Prehuman Times to the French Revolution. Farrar, Straus and Giroux. 2012

Garrison, Roger: Time and Money: The Macroeconomics of Capital Structure (Routledge Foundations of the Market Economy) New Edition. Routledge 2007

Gatto, John Taylor: The Underground History of American Education, Volume I: An Intimate Investigation Into the Prison of Modern Schooling. Valor Academy 2017

Guerin, Daniel (ed.): No Gods No Masters: An Anthology of Anarchism. AK Press 2005

Giddens, Anthony: The Third Way: The Renewal of Social Democracy. Polity Press. 1999

Giddens, Anthony: Capitalism and Modern Social Theory: An Analysis of the Writings of Marx, Durkheim and Max Weber. Cambridge University Press. 1973

Goodwin, Barbara: Justice by Lottery (Sortition and Public Policy). Imprint Academic 2005

Gordon, Robert J. : The Rise and Fall of American Growth: The U.S. Standard of Living since the Civil War (The Princeton Economic History of the Western World). Princeton University Press 2017

Gordon, David: An Austro-Libertarian View: Current Affairs, Foreign Policy, American History, European History (Essays by David Gordon). 3 vols. The Ludwig von Mises Institute. 2017

Granovetter, Marc: Society and Economy: Framework and Principles. Belknap Press: An Imprint of Harvard University Press. 2017

Grant, James: The Forgotten Depression: 1921: The Crash That Cured Itself. Simon & Schuster. 2014

Greenspan, Alan with Adrian Wooldridge: Capitalism in America. A History. Penguin Press 2018

Greenspan, Alan: The Age of Turbulence: Adventures in a New World. Penguin Books 2008

Halberstam, Davin: The Best and the Brightest. Modern Library. 2002

Harford, Tim: Fifty Inventions that Shaped the Modern Economy. Riverhead Books. 2017

Harris, Fred and Alan Curtis (eds.): Healing Our Divided Society: Investing in America Fifty Years after the Kerner Report. Temple University Press. 2018

Haskel, Jonathan and Stian Westlake: Capitalism without Capital: The Rise of the Intangible. Princeton University Press. 2017

Hathaway, Oona A. and Scott J. Shapiro: The Internationalists: How a Radical Plan to Outlaw War Remade the World. Simon & Schuster. 2017

Hayek, Friedrich A. von: Individualism and Economic Order. University of Chicago Press. 1996

Hayek, Friedrich A. von: The Constitution of Liberty: The Definitive Edition (The Collected Works of F. A. Hayek). University of Chicago Press. 2011

Hayek, Friedrich A. von: The Road to Serfdom: Text and Documents -The Definitive Edition (The Collected Works of F. A. Hayek, Volume 2). University of Chicago Press. 2007

Hayek, Friedrich A.: Denationalisation of Money. The Argument Refined. CreateSpace Independent Publishing Platform. 2014

Hazlitt, Henry: Economics in One Lesson: The Shortest and Surest Way to Understand Basic Economics. Crown Business. 1988

Hazlitt, Henry: The Failure of the New Economics. Martino Fine Books. 2016

Heidegger, Martin: The Question Concerning Technology, and Other Essays (Harper Perennial Modern Thought). Harper Perennial Modern Classics; Reissue edition. 2013

Hennig, Brett: The End of Politicians: Time for a Real Democracy. Unbound Digital. 2017

Herbener, Jeffrey M. : Pure Time-Preference Theory of Interest. Ludwig von Mises Institute. 2011

Heyne, Paul L., Peter J. Boettke, and David L. Prychito: The Economic Way of Thinking. Pearson Series in Economics. 2013

Hicks, Stephen, R. C.: Explaining Postmodernism: Skepticism and Socialism from Rousseau to Foucault (Expanded Edition). Ockham's Razor Publishers. 2011

Higgs, Robert: Against Leviathan: Government Power and a Free Society (Independent Studies in Political Economy). Independent Institute. 2004

Higgs, Robert: Crisis and Leviathan: Critical Episodes in the Growth of American Government, 25th Anniversary Edition (Independent Studies in Political Economy). Independent Institute; Anniversary edition. 2013

Higgs, Robert: Depression, War, and Cold War: Studies in Political Economy. Oxford University Press. 2006

Higgs, Robert: Taking a Stand: Reflections on Life, Liberty, and the Economy. Independent Institute. 2015

Hirschman, Albert O.: The Passions and the Interests. Political Arguments before its Triumph (Princeton Classics). Princeton University. 2013

Hirschmann, Albert O.: Exit, Voice, and Loyalty: Responses to Decline in Firms, Organizations, and States. Harvard University Press 1970

Holcombe, Randall G.: Advanced Introduction to Public Choice (Elgar Advanced Introductions series). Edward Elgar Publishers. 2016

Holcombe, Randall G.: Advanced Introduction to the Austrian School of Economics (Elgar Advanced Introductions series). Edgar Elgar Publishers. 2014

Holcombe, Randall G.: Producing Prosperity: An Inquiry into the Operation of the Market Process (Routledge Foundations of the Market Economy). Routledge 2015

Holcombe, Randall G.: Entrepreneurship and Economic Progress (Routledge Foundations of the Market Economy). Routledge 2006

Hoppe, Hans-Hermann: A Short History of Man: Progress and Decline. Ludwig von Mises Institute 2015

Hoppe, Hans-Hermann: A Theory of Socialism and Capitalism. Ludwig von Mises Institute. 2003

Hoppe, Hans-Hermann: Democracy. The God that Failed: Economics and Politics of Monarchy, Democracy and Natural Order (Perspectives on Democratic Practice. Routledge. 2001

Hoppe, Hans-Hermann: The Economics and Ethics of Private Property: Studies in Political Economy and Philosophy, 2nd Edition. Ludwig von Mises Institute. 2010

Hoppe, Hans-Herman: The Myth of National Defense: Essays on the Theory and History of Security Production. Ludwig von Mises Institute. 2003

Horwitz, Steve: Hayek's Modern Family: Classical Liberalism and the Evolution of Social Institutions. Palgrave Macmillan. 2015

Howden, David and Joseph T. Salerno (eds.): The Fed at One Hundred: A Critical View on the Federal Reserve System. Springer. 2014

Huebert, Jacob H.: Libertarianism Today. Praeger 2010

Huerta de Soto, Jesus: Money, Bank Credit, and Economic Cycles. Ludwig von Mises Institute. 2012

Hülsmann, Jörg Guido and Stephan Kinsella (eds.): Property, Freedom, and Society: Essays in Honor of Hans-Hermann Hoppe (LvMI). Ludwig von Mises Institute 2011

Hülsmann, Jörg Guido: The Ethics of Money Production. Ludwig von Mises Institute. 2008

Humboldt, Wilhelm von: The Sphere and Duties of Government (The Limits of State Action). Martino Fine Books. 2014

Illich, Ivan: Deschooling Society (Open Forum S). Marion Boyars Publishers Ltd; New edition edition. 2000

Illich, Ivan: Limits to Medicine: Medical Nemesis, the Expropriation of Health. Marion Boyars Publishers Ltd; Revised ed. Edition. 2000

Infantino, Lorenzo: Individualism in Modern Thought: From Adam Smith to Hayek (Routledge Studies in Social and Political Thought). Routledge 2014

Irwin, Douglas A.: Against the Tide. An Intellectual History of Free Trade. Princeton University Press. 1996

Joshi, Vijay: India's Long Road: The Search for Prosperity. Oxford University Press. 2017

Juma, Calestous: Innovation and Its Enemies: Why People Resist New Technologies. Oxford University Press. 2016

Kant, Imanuel and H.S. Reiss (ed). Kant: Political Writings (Cambridge Texts in the History of Political Thought). Cambridge University Press. 1991

Kealey, Terence: The Case Against Public Science. Cato Unbound. August 2013

Kealey, Terence: The Economic Laws of Scientific Research. Palgrave Macmillan. 1996

Kengor, Paul: The Politically Incorrect Guide to Communism (The Politically Incorrect Guides). Regnery Publishing 2017

Kenny, Charles: Getting Better: Why Global Development Is Succeeding - And How We Can Improve the World Even More. Basic Books. 2012

Keynes, John Maynard: The General Theory of Employment, Interest and Money: With the Economic Consequences of the Peace (Classics of World Literature). Wordworth Editions 2017

Kinsella, Stephan: Against Intellectual Property. Ludwig von Mises Institute. 2015

Kirzner, Israel: Competition and Entrepreneurship (The Collected Works of Israel M. Kirzner). Liberty Fund. 2013
Knight, Frank: Risk, Uncertainty and Profit. Martino Fine Books. 2014
Kocka, Jürgen: Capitalism. A Short History. Princeton University Press. 2017
Kroeber, Arthur A.: China's Economy: What Everyone Needs to Know. Oxford University Press. 2016
Kuehnelt-Leddihn: Eric Ritter von: Liberty or Equality: The Challenge of Our Times. The Ludwig von Mises Institute. 2014
Kuehnelt-Leddihn: Eric Ritter von: Menace of the Herd or Procrustes at Large. Ludwig von Mises Institute. 2012
Kurer, Oskar: John Stuart Mill (Routledge Revivals): The Politics of Progress. Routledge 2018
Kurer, Oskar: The Political Foundations of Development Policies. UPA Publishers 1996
Kurlansky, Mark: Nonviolence: The History of a Dangerous Idea (Modern Library Chronicles). Modern Library 2008
Kurzweil, Ray: The Singularity Is Near: When Humans Transcend Biology. Penguin Books. 2006
Lavoie, Don: Rivalry and Central Planning. The Socialist Calculation Debate Reconsidered (Advanced Studies in Political Economy). Mercatus Center at George Mason University. 2015
Leeson, Peter: Anarchy Unbound: Why Self-Governance Works Better Than You Think (Cambridge Studies in Economics, Choice, and Society). Cambridge University Press. 2014
Leonard, Thomas C.: Illiberal Reformers: Race, Eugenics, and American Economics in the Progressive Era. Princeton University Press. 2017
Legutko, Ryszard: The Demon in Democracy: Totalitarian Temptations in Free Societies. Encounter Books. 2016
Lenin, Vladimir Ilich: State and Revolution. Martino Fine Books. 2011
Leoni, Bruno: Freedom and the Law. Liberty Fund. 1991
Lerch, Hubert: An Introduction to Political Philosophy. CreateSpace Independent Publishing Platform. 2011
Levin, Mark R.: Rediscovering Americanism: And the Tyranny of Progressivism. Threshold Editions. 2017
Levitsky, Steven and Daniel Zieblatt: How Democracies Die. Crown 2018
Lewis, Hunter: Economics in Three Lessons and One Hundred Economics Laws: Two Works in One Volume. Axios Press. 2017
Lewis, Hunter: Where Keynes Went Wrong: And Why World Governments Keep Creating Inflation, Bubbles, and Busts. Axios Press. 2009
Lilla, Mark: The Once and Future Liberal: After Identity Politics. Harper. 2017
Lindsay, Brink: The Age of Abundance: How Prosperity Transformed America's Politics and Culture. Harper Business Reprint edition. 2008

Lingle, Christopher: The Rise and Decline of the Asian Century: False Starts on the Path to the Global Millennium. Bookworld Services. 1998

Lingle, Christopher: The Rise and Decline of the Asian Century: False Starts on the Path to the Global Millennium. Bookworld Services. 1998

Machaj, Mateusz: Money, Interest, and the Structure of Production: Resolving Some Puzzles in the Theory of Capital (Capitalist Thought: Studies in Philosophy, Politics, and Economics). Lexington Books. 2017

Mallaby, Sebastian: The Man Who Knew: The Life and Times of Alan Greenspan. Penguin Books. 2017

Maltsev, Yuri: Requiem for Marx. CreateSpace Independent Publishing Platform. 1993

Maltsev, Yuri: Mass Murder and Public Slavery: The Soviet Experience. The Independent Review 2017

Mandeville, Bernard: The Fable of the Bees and Other Writings (Hackett Classics). Hacket Publishing Company. 1997

Marx, Karl: Das Kapital: A Critique of Political Economy. CreateSpace Independent Publishing Platform. 2011

Marx, Karl and Friedrich Engels: The Communist Manifesto. International Publishers Co; New edition. 2014

McCaffrey, Matthew: The Economic Theory of Costs: Foundations and New Directions (Routledge Frontiers of Political Economy). Routledge 2017

McCloskey, Deirdre: The Bourgeois Virtues: Ethics for an Age of Commerce. University of Chicago Press. 2007

McGroarty, Emmett, Jane Robbins, and Erin Tuttle: Deconstructing the Administrative State. Liberty Hill Publishing. 2017

McLuhan, Marshall: The Gutenberg Galaxy. University of Toronto Press, Scholarly Publishing Division. 2011

Menger, Carl: Principles of Economics. CreateSpace Independent Publishing Platform. 2007

Mencken, H. L.: Notes on Democracy. CreateSpace Independent Publishing Platform. 2013

Mesquita, Bruce Bueno de and Alistair Smith: The Dictator's Handbook: Why Bad Behavior is Almost Always Good Politics. PublicAffairs. 2012

Mierzejewski, Alfred C.: Ludwig Erhard: A Biography. University of North Carolina Press. 2014

Mill, John Stuart: On Liberty, Utilitarianism and Other Essays (Oxford World's Classics). Cambridge University Press. 2015

Miller, Tom: China's Asian Dream: Empire Building along the New Silk Road. Zed Books. 2017

Mises, Ludwig von: Human Action. The Scholar's Edition. Ludwig von Mises Institute. 2010

Mises, Ludwig von: Liberalism. Liberty Fund. 2005

Mises, Ludwig von: Economic Calculation in the Socialist Commonwealth. Ludwig von Mises Institute. 2012

Mises, Ludwig von: Interventionism: An Economic Analysis (Lib Works Ludwig Von Mises PB). Liberty Fund. 2011

Mokyr, Joel: A Culture of Growth: The Origins of the Modern Economy (Graz Schumpeter Lectures). Princeton University Press 2016

Mokyr, Joel: Gift of Athena: Historical Origins of the Knowledge Economy. Princeton University Press 2014

Mokyr, Joel: The Lever of Riches: Technological Creativity and Economic Progress. Oxford University Press. 1992

Molyneux, Stefan: Practical Anarchy. The Freedom of the Future. CreateSpace Independent Publishing Platform. 2017

Mueller, Antony P.: Bubble or New Era? Monetary Aspects of the New Economy. in: Birner, Jack and Pierre Garrouste (eds): Markets, Information and Communication: Austrian Perspectives on the Internet Economy (Routledge Foundations of the Market Economy). Routledge. 2003, pp. 249-261

Muller, Jerry Z.: The Tyranny of Metrics. Princeton University Press. 2018

Muller, Jerry Z.: The Mind and the Market: Capitalism in Western Thought. Anchor. 2003

Murphy, Robert: The Politically Incorrect Guide to the Great Depression and the New Deal (The Politically Incorrect Guides). Regnery Publishing. 2009

Murphy, Robert: Choice: Cooperation, Enterprise, and Human Action. Independent Institute. 2015

Molinari, Gustave de: The Production of Security. Edited by Richard Ebeling with an Introduction by Murray Rothbard. Create Space. 2009

Murray, Charles: In Our Hands: A Plan to Replace the Welfare State. AEI Press. 2016

Murray, Charles: By the People: Rebuilding Liberty Without Permission. Crown Forum. 2015

Murray, Charles: Losing Ground: American Social Policy, 1950-1980. Basic Books. 2015

Nietzsche, Friedrich: The Will to Power. Independently published. 2017

Niskanen, William A.: Reaganomics: An Insider's Account of the Policies and the People. Oxford University Press. 1988

Norberg, Johan: Ten Reasons to Look Forward to the Future. Oneworld Publication. 2017

North, Douglas C. and Robert Paul Thomas: The Rise of the Western World: A New Economic History. Cambridge University Press. 1976

North, Douglass C.: Institutions, Institutional Change and Economic Performance (Political Economy of Institutions and Decisions) Cambridge University Press. 1990

North, Gary: Mises on Money. Ludwig von Mises Institute. 2012

Novak, Michael and Paul Adams: Social Justice Isn't What You Think It Is. Encounter Books. 2015

Nozick, Robert: Anarchy, State, and Utopia. Basic Books Reprint. 2013

O'Driscoll, Gerald P. and Maria Rizzo: The Economics of Time and Ignorance. Routledge Foundations of the Market Economy. Routledge 1996

OECD (Organization for Economic Cooperation and Development: The Sources of Economic Growth in OECD Countries. OECD 2003

Oliver, Michael J.: The New Libertarianism: Anarcho-Capitalism. CreateSpace. 2013

Olson, Mancur: The Logic of Collective Action. Public Goods and the Theory of Groups. Second printing with new preface and appendix (Harvard Economic Studies). Harvard University Press. 1971

Oppenheimer, Franz: The State: Its History and Development Viewed Sociologically. (Classic Reprint). Forgotten Books. 2012

O'Rourke, P. J.: Parliament of Whores: A Lone Humorist Attempts to Explain the Entire U.S. Government. Grove Press. 2003

O'Rourke, P. J.: Eat the Rich: A Treatise on Economics. Atlantic Monthly Press. 1999

Ortega y Gasset, José: The Revolt of the Masses. W. W. Norten & Company. 1994

Ostrom, Elinor: Governing the Commons: The Evolution of Institutions for Collective Action (Canto Classics). Cambridge University Press; Reissue edition. 2015

Ostrowski, James: Progressivism: A Primer on the Idea Destroying America. Cazenovia Books. 2014

Palmer, Tom: Realizing Freedom: Libertarian Theory, History, and Practice. Cato Institute. 2014

Palmer, Tom G, Virginia Prostel, Brink Lindsey, and Tyler Cowen: Libertarianism. Past and Prospects (Cato Unbound Book 32007). Cato Institute. 2007

Parijs, Philippe Van and Yannick Vanderborght: Basic Income: A Radical Proposal for a Free Society and a Sane Economy. Harvard University Press. 2017

Paul, Ron: End the Fed. Grand Central Publishing. 2010

Paul, Ron: Revolution. A Manifesto. Grand Central Publishing. 2009

Pesek, William: Japanization: What the World Can Learn from Japan's Lost Decades. Wiley 2014

Phelps, Edmund: Mass Flourishing. How Grassroots Innovation Creates Jobs, Challenge, and Change. Princeton University Press. 2015

Pilling, David: The Growth Delusion: Wealth, Poverty, and the Well-Being of Nations. Tim Duggan Books. 2018

Pinker, Steven: Enlightenment Now: The Case for Reason, Science, Humanism, and Progress. Viking 2018

Pinker, Steven: The Better Angels of Our Nature: Why Violence Has Declined. Penguin Books. 2012

Postrel, Virginia: The Future and Its Enemies: The Growing Conflict Over Creativity, Enterprise. Free Press. 2011

Powell, Benjamin: Out of Poverty: Sweatshops in the Global Economy (Cambridge Studies in Economics, Choice, and Society). Cambridge University Press. 2014

Powell, Jim: FDR's Folly: How Roosevelt and His New Deal Prolonged the Great Depression. Crown Forum. 2004

Powell, James and Paul Johnson: The Triumph of Liberty: A 2,000 Year History Told Through the Lives of Freedom's Greatest Champions. Free Press. 2000

Qui, Insula: Capitalism Works. Independently published. 2018

Rachels, Chase and Christopher Chase Rachels: A Spontaneous Order: The Capitalist Case for a Stateless Society. CreateSpace Independent Publishing Platform. 2015

Raico, Ralph: Classical Liberalism and the Austrian School. CreateSpace Independent Publishing Platform. 2012

Raico, Ralph: Great Wars and Great Leaders: A Libertarian Rebuttal. Ludwig von Mises Institute. 2015

Ratner-Rosenhagen, Jennifer: American Nietzsche: A History of an Icon and His Ideas. University of Chicago Press; Reprint edition. 2012

Rawls, John: Justice as Fairness: A Restatement. Belknap Press: An Imprint of Harvard University Press. 2001

Rand, Ayn: Capitalism. The Unknown Ideal. Signet; Reissue edition. 1986

Reed, Lawrence R.: Great Myth of the Great Depression. Foundation for Economic Education. 2015

Reisman, George: Capitalism. A Treatise on Economics. TJS Books 1996

Reisman, George: The Government Against the Economy. Jameson Books. 1985

Reybrouck, David van: Against Elections. The Case for Democracy. Random House U.K. 2017

Reynolds, Morgan O.: Making America Poorer: The Cost of Labor Law. Cato Institute. 1987

Richman, Sheldon: America's Counter-Revolution: The Constitution Revisited. Grifien & Lash. 2016

Ridley, Matt: The Rational Optimist: How Prosperity Evolves. Harper Perennial. 2011

Rifkin, Jeremy: The Zero Marginal Cost Society: The Internet of Things, the Collaborative Commons, and the Eclipse of Capitalism. St. Martin's Griffin; Reprint edition. 2015

Ritenour, Shawn (ed.): The Mises Reader Unabridged. Ludwig von Mises Institute. 2016

Roberts, Paul Craig: The Tyranny of Good Intentions: How Prosecutors and Law Enforcement Are Trampling the Constitution in the Name of Justice. Crown. 2008

Rockwell, Llewellyn, H. Jr.: Against the State. An Anarcho-Capitalist Manifesto. Rockwell Communication. 2014

Rosenberg, Nathan and L. E. Birdzell: How the West Grew Rich: The Economic Transformation Of The Industrial World. Basic Books. 1987

Rosling, Hans, Anna Rosling Rönnlund, Ola Rosling: Factfulness: Ten Reasons We're Wrong About the World--and Why Things Are Better Than You Think. Flatiron Books 2018

Rothbard, Murray N.: Anatomy of the State. Bhpublishing. 2014

Rothbard, Murray N.: For a New Liberty. The Libertarian Manifesto. CreateSpace Independent Publishing Platform. 2006

Rothbard, Murray N.: What Has Government Done to Our Money? Ludwig von Mises Institute. 2015

Rothbard, Murray N.: Man, Economy, and State with Power and Market, Scholar's Edition. Ludwig von Mises Institute. 2011

Rothbard, Murray N.: America's Great Depression. Ludwig von Mises Institute. 2000

Rummel, Rudy J.: Death by Government: Genocide and Mass Murder Since 1900. Routledge 1997

Rummel, Rudy J.: The Blue Book of Freedom: Ending Famine, Poverty, Democide, and War. Cumberland House Publishing. 2007

Salerno, Joseph T.: Money: Sound and Unsound. Ludwig von Mises Institute. 2015

Say, Jean-Baptiste: A Treatise on Political Economy: Or the Production, Distribution and Consumption of Wealth. CreateSpace Independent Publishing Platform. 2013

Schiff, Peter: How an Economy Grows and Why It Crashes. Wiley. 2010

Schmitt, Carl: The Leviathan in the State Theory of Thomas Hobbes: Meaning and Failure of a Political Symbol (Heritage of Sociology). University of Chicago Press Ed Edition. 2008

Schmitt, Carl: The Concept of the Political: Expanded Edition Enlarged Edition with a Commentary by Leo Strauss. The University of Chicago Press. 2007

Schoolland, Ken: The Adventures of Jonathan Gullible. A Free Market Odyssey. Liberty Publishing. 2011

Schumpeter, Joseph A.: Business Cycles: A Theoretical, Historical, and Statistical Analysis of the Capitalist Process (2 Vols.). Martino Fine Books. 2017

Schumpeter, Joseph A.: Can Capitalism Survive?: Creative Destruction and the Future of the Global Economy. Harper Perennial Modern Classics. 2009

Schumpeter, Joseph A.: Capitalism, Socialism, and Democracy: Third Edition. Harper Perennial Modern Classics. 2008

Schumpeter, Joseph A.: Essays: On Entrepreneurs, Innovations, Business Cycles and the Evolution of Capitalism. Routledge 1989

Schumpeter, Joseph A.: Theory of Economic Development (Social Science Classics Series). Routledge 1981

Schwab, Klaus and Nicholas Davis, Satya Nadella: Shaping the Fourth Industrial Revolution. World Economic Forum. 2018

Scruton, Roger: Fools, Frauds and Firebrands: Thinkers of the New Left. Bloomsbury Continuum. 2017

Selgin, George: Financial Stability without Central Banks. London Publishing Partnership. 2018

Selgin, George: Money: Free and Unfree. Cato Institute. 2017

Selgin, George: Less Than Zero. The Case for a Falling Price Level in a Growing Economy. CreateSpace Independent Publishing Platform. 2014

Selgin, George: The Theory of Free Banking. Rowman & Littlefield Publisher. 1988

Sen, Amartya: Development as Freedom. Anchor. 2000

Sévillia, Jean: Le terrorisme intellectuel (French Edition). Tempus Perrain. 2017

Shaffer, Butler: Boundaries of Order: Private Property as a Social System. CreateSpace Independent Publishing Platform. 2009

Shaffer, Buttler: The Wizards of Ozymandias: Reflections on the Decline and Fall. CreateSpace Independent Publishing Platform. 2012

Shlae, Amity: The Forgotten Man: A New History of the Great Depression Harper Perennial. 2008

Simon, Julian Lincoln: The Ultimate Resource 2. Princeton University Press. 1998

Sintomer, Yves: Das demokratische Experiment: Geschichte des Losverfahrens in der Politik von Athen bis heute (German Edition). Springer 2016

Smiley, Gene: Rethinking the Great Depression (American Ways). Ivan R. Dee Publisher. 2003

Smith, Adam: The Theory of Moral Sentiments. Digireads.com. 2010

Smith, Adam: The Wealth of Nations (Bantam Classics). Bantam Classics; Annotated edition. 2003

Snyder, Timothy: On Tyranny: Twenty Lessons from the Twentieth Century. Tim Duggan Books. 2017

Sombart, Werner: The Quintessence Of Capitalism: A Study Of The History And Psychology Of The Modern Business Man. Scholar Select. Andesite Press. 2017

Solzhenitsyn, Aleksandr: The Gulag Archipelago. The Harvill Press. 2003

Soto, Hernando de: The Mystery of Capital: Why Capitalism Triumphs in the West and Fails Everywhere Else. Basic Books. 2003

Sowell, Thomas: Basic Economics. Basic Books. 2014

Sowell, Thomas: Economic Facts and Fallacies. Basic Books. 2011

Sowell, Thomas: The Quest for Cosmic Justice. Free Press 2002

Spencer, Herbert: Social Statics: Or, The Conditions Essential to Human Happiness Specified and the First of them Developed. Nabu Press. 2011

Srinivasa, Bhu: Americana: A 400-Year History of American Capitalism. Penguin Press. 2017

Steil, Ben: The Marshall Plan: Dawn of the Cold War. Simon & Schuster. 2018

Steil, Ben: The Battle of Bretton Woods: John Maynard Keynes, Harry Dexter White, and the Making of a New World Order (Council on Foreign Relations Books). Princeton University Press. 2014

Stirner, Max: The Ego and His Own: The Case of the Individual Against Authority (Dover Books on Western Philosophy). Dover Publications. 2005

Stone, Peter: Lotteries in Public Life: A Reader (Sortition and Public Policy). Imprint Academic. 2012

Stringham, Edward Peter: Private Governance: Creating Order in Economic and Social Life. Oxford University Press. 2015

Susskind, Richard and Daniel Susskind: The Future of the Professions: How Technology Will Transform the Work of Human Experts. Oxford University Press. Reprint edition. 2017

Suvorov, Viktor: Icebreaker. Who Started the Second World War? PL UK Publishing. 2012

Taleb, Nassim Nicholas: Skin in the Game: Hidden Asymmetries in Daily Life. Random House 2018

Taylor, Frederick: The Downfall of Money: Germany's Hyperinflation and the Destruction of the Middle Class. Bloomsbury Press. 2015

Taylor, Mark Zachary: The Politics of Innovation: Why Some Countries Are Better Than Others at Science and Technology. Oxford University Press. 2016

Thiel, Peter: Zero to One: Notes on Startups, or How to Build the Future. Currency Publishers. 2014

Thornton, Mark: The Bastiat Collection. Ludwig von Mises Institute. 2017

Thornton, Mark: The Economics of Prohibition. Ludwig von Mises Institute. 2014

Tilly, Charles: Coercion, Capital and European States, A.D. 990 - 1992. Wiley-Blackwell. 1992

Tirole, Jean: Economics for the Common Good. Princeton University Press. 2017

Tooley, Hunt: The Great War: Western Front and Home Front. Palgrave 2015

Tucker, Jeffrey: A Beautiful Anarchy: How to Create Your Own Civilization in the Digital Age. Laissez Faire Books. 2012

Vance, Laurence M.: War, Empire, and the Military: Essays on the Follies of War and U.S. Foreign Policy. Vance Publications. 2014

Vedder, Richard: Going Broke By Degree: Why College Cost. AEI Press. 2004

Veryser, Harry C.: It Didn't Have to be This Way: Why Boom and Bust Is Unncessary - and How the Austrian School of Economics Breaks the Cycle (Culture of Enterprise).ISI Books.2013

Volcker, Paul with Christine Harper: Keeping At It. The Quest for Sound Money and Good Government. PublicAffairs. 2018

Volcker, Paul with Christine Harper: Keeping At It. The Quest for Sound Money and Good Government. PublicAffairs. 2018

Volcker, Paul and Toyoo Gyohten. Changing Fortunes. Crown. 1992

Walsh, Michael: The Devil's Pleasure Palace: The Cult of Critical Theory and the Subversion of the West. Encounter Books. 2017

White, Lawrence: The Clash of Economic Ideas: The Great Policy Debates and Experiments of the Last Hundred Years. Cambridge University Press. 2012

White, Lawrence: The Theory of Monetary Institutions. Wiley-Blackwell. 1999

White, Lawrence: Competition and Currency: Essays on Free Banking and Money. New York University Press. 1992

Wisniewski, Jakub: The Economics of Law, Order, and Action: The Logic of Public Goods (Routledge Advances in Heterodox Economics). Routledge. 2018

Williams, Walter E.: American Contempt for Liberty (Hoover Institution Press Publication). Hoover Institution Press 2015 Williams, Walter E.: Race & Economics: How Much Can Be Blamed on Discrimination?. Hoover Institution Press. 2011

Wolfram, Gary: A Capitalist Manifesto: Understanding The Market Economy And Defending Liberty. Dunlap Goddard. 2013

Woods, Thomas E.: Meltdown: A Free-Market Look at Why the Stock Market Collapsed, the Economy Tanked, and Government Bailouts Will Make Things Worse. Regnery 2009

Yergin, Daniel and Joseph Stanislaw: The Commanding Heights: The Battle for the World Economy. Free Press. 2002

Zelmanovitz, Leonidas: The Ontology and Function of Money: The Philosophical Fundamentals of Monetary Institutions (Capitalist Thought: Studies in Philosophy, Politics, and Economics). Lexington Books 2015

Antony P. Mueller

ABOUT THE AUTHOR

Antony P. Mueller is a German professor of economics who currently teaches at the Federal University UFS in Brazil where he also serves in the graduate and doctoral programs in economics and sociology. He holds a doctorate in economics from the Friedrich-Alexander University Erlangen-Nuremberg, Germany.
Contact:
antonymueller@gmx.com
*See his Amazon author page:*https://www.amazon.com/ANTONY-P.-MUELLER/e/B07BHF4RG8/ref=ntt_dp_epwbk_0

RELATED BOOKS

Beyond the State and Politics. Capitalism for the New Millennium. Amazon KDP 2018

ISBN-10: 1717773761
ISBN-13: 978-1717773760

Capitalism Beyond the State and Politics. Expanded textbook edition. Amazon KDP 2018

ISBN-10: 1717759890
ISBN-13: 978-1717759894

THE DEBACLE OF ECONOMIC STABILIZATION POLICIES

www.ingramcontent.com/pod-product-compliance
Lightning Source LLC
Chambersburg PA
CBHW031424210526
45464CB00005B/2047